LOVE AND MARRIAGE PERSPECTIVES

Strategies and Skills to Consider in Building a Successful, Lasting Marriage

VINCE BRENDAN VINCENTS

Outskirts Press, Inc.
Denver, Colorado

The opinions expressed in this manuscript are solely the opinions of the author and do not represent the opinions or thoughts of the publisher. The author has represented and warranted full ownership and/or legal right to publish all the materials in this book.

Love and Marriage Perspectives
Strategies and Skills to Consider in Building a Successful Lasting Marriage
All Rights Reserved.
Copyright © 2011 Vince Brendan Vincents
v2.0

Cover Photo © 2011 JupiterImages Corporation. All rights reserved - used with permission.

This book may not be reproduced, transmitted, or stored in whole or in part by any means, including graphic, electronic, or mechanical without the express written consent of the publisher except in the case of brief quotations embodied in critical articles and reviews.

Outskirts Press, Inc.
http://www.outskirtspress.com

PB ISBN: 978-1-4327-7429-5
HB ISBN: 978-1-4327-7458-5

Library of Congress Control Number: 2011926898

Outskirts Press and the "OP" logo are trademarks belonging to Outskirts Press, Inc.

PRINTED IN THE UNITED STATES OF AMERICA

To my parents, Charles and Cordelia, of blessed memory, and to couples all over the world in their quest to understand this mystery called marriage.

Table of Contents

Author's Notes i

Acknowledgments iii

Introduction v

Chapter One: Nuts And Bolts Of Selecting A Spouse 1

Chapter Two: Being In Love, Staying In Love,
And Growing In Love 25

Chapter Three: Building And Maintaining Marriages 57

Chapter Four: The Husband And The Wife 93

Chapter Five: The Family—Customs, Traditions,
And Roles 123

Chapter Six: Communication Styles In Marriages 141

Chapter Seven: Sexual Attitudes, Patterns,
And Exclusivity In Marriage 155

Chapter Eight: Resolving Marital Conflicts 169

Chapter Nine: Prayer And Marriage 179

Chapter Ten: Marital Stress 209

Chapter Eleven: Anger In Marriage 235

Chapter Twelve: Attitude in Marriage 261

Chapter Thirteen: Spousal Abuse 279

Chapter Fourteen: Divorce 293

Chapter Fifteen: Forgiveness 305

Concluding Remarks 321

Author's Notes

NAMES USED IN this book are fictional and in no way represent or portray any actual person in the story or stories. It should be further noted that histories or stories herein are for illustrative purposes, solely for facilitating the understanding of issues or presentations in this book. They should in no way be interpreted or misconstrued to be true stories.

Opinions expressed in this book are solely mine and any errors are also mine.

All Biblical quotations included herein are from the Holy Bible, New King James Version (1990), by Thomas Nelson Publishers, Nashville, unless otherwise indicated at the end of the quotation.

Acknowledgments

WRITING THIS BOOK is a good example of how people are interdependent—no one is an island.

I am grateful to my parents for instilling in me the true meaning of hard work and the importance of completing a difficult task in trying situations. In addition to my parents, Charles and Cordelia, Pauline became that glimmer of hope and the catalyst that spurred and jolted me to action when all hope appeared lost concerning this manuscript. If not for her incessant support, courage, and encouragement, I probably would not have completed this manuscript.

Three individuals typed this manuscript, and I am very grateful to all of them for their efforts toward this manuscript.

I am lucky to have two outstanding specialists on this project. They are Jodee Thayer my publishing consultant and Ellen Nollenberger, Title Production Supervisor. They are both professionals to the core. Not only are they assets to outskirts press, they have always responded quickly and enthusiastically to my publishing needs.

LOVE AND MARRIAGE PERSPECTIVES

I have friends and associates who are not mentioned by name. Suffice it to say that I am grateful to each and every one of you for your respective contributions to my life.

Vince Brendan Vincents

Introduction

THE OBJECTIVE OF *Love and Marriage Perspectives* is to take couples on a journey through most attributes of marriage. This journey will be undertaken in stages. There can be great emotional enrichment and attachment in marriage. There can also be marital discontent and discord. The extent to which these issues affect marriages depends on the couples undertaking this journey, and their constitutional makeup as far as personality. Have you sometimes pondered the following?

- Why do some marriages fail and others succeed?

- Why are some couples in troubled and conflict-ridden marriages, yet some are in fulfilling marriages?

- What are the necessary skills needed to cope with marital challenges without overreacting?

In order to make their own marital relationships worthwhile, how can couples learn from the mistakes or the successes of others who have been down this path?

Most marriages begin to form at the dating or courtship stage.

LOVE AND MARRIAGE PERSPECTIVES

This stage is a prelude to the point at which the rubber meets the road, in that the intended spouses have an opportunity to learn all about each other. That is where you explore just who this individual is whom you are dating and may possibly marry. Things to think about include:

- (1) What type of personality does he have? *— Short tempered, Pride*

- Will he open doors for you? *— Vulgar language, Disrespects women*

- How does he resolve conflicts? *— With anger, Blame game*

- What type of attitude does he exhibit in situations? *— He is always right, does not listen to others.*

- How does he resolve conflicts?

- What type of communication pattern does he have? *one-way communication. Include others.*

- Does he engage in active or passive listening?

- How will he feel about his intended in-laws? *He does not care.*

This is the stage to know if Mr. Right or Ms. Right is really right for you.

Love and Marriage Perspectives ventures into what love is by exploring how to be in love, grow in love, and stay in love. Since love means different things to different people, it is incumbent on the

INTRODUCTION

spouses-to-be to find out at this point if their own definition of love is met in this relationship. Marriage requires skills to cope with issues emanating from its daily activities and interactions. That fact prompted this author to discuss coping mechanisms such as those that follow:

- The need to communicate in marriages
- Impact of anger on marriages
- How attitude affects marriage
- Stress management
- How to resolve marital conflicts

The intention of such discussion is to enable couples to be armed with those tools when needed, thereby building a healthy and successful marriage. Couples are offered alternatives and strategies with the objective of addressing behaviors that are regressing the marriage. When feelings are expressed impulsively and without forethought, they negatively impact marriages.

Marriage is often full of happiness, but that happiness can sometimes be punctuated with sadness. In other words, marriage is not always a bed of roses. Spousal abuse and even divorce are factors in some marriages. *Love and Marriage Perspectives* further delves into those issues with techniques to ponder during those times.

LOVE AND MARRIAGE PERSPECTIVES

There is also the issue of forgiveness. In this regard, the author took into account that because a husband and wife are human, there are bound to be human weaknesses, mistakes, and frailties.

Sexual exclusivity is encouraged, for it results in marital happiness and harmony, and it gives more meaning to the contract and covenant of marriage. Sex is one of the fringe benefits of marriage, further acting as glue that binds couples together.

This author has seen the exhilarating aspects and problems of adjustment in marriages. He worked as a caseworker in a state school, where he did individual, group, and family counseling. He was also a therapist at a group home. In that capacity, he facilitated individual, family, and group therapy. The author worked privately as a social worker and a chemical dependency counselor. Prior to writing full time, he was a vocational rehabilitation counselor. As a divorced person after many years of marriage, he brings a balanced perspective by combining his professional and personal experience in marital issues. As an ordained minister, the author believes that marriages are salvageable through forgiveness, reconciliation, and contrition. This, however, depends on the willingness of the individuals involved in the marriages to go through the stages of forgiveness and exhibit the spirit of contrition. Personalities of the individuals in a relationship and their propensity to forgive are important determining factors in this regard. The Lord's Prayer states in part, "Forgive us our trespasses as we forgive those who trespass against us," and so shall we forgive in marriage, in that we are one flesh with our spouse.

CHAPTER ONE

Nuts And Bolts Of Selecting A Spouse

Don't marry someone you can live with. Marry someone you can't live without.

—Josh McDowell

SELECTING A MATE is a complex phenomenon. The reason is that a lot of thought and consideration goes toward the process. A solid marriage starts with a solid foundation and a good plan. The key element to your marriage is a good spouse. This is where your selection process comes into play. Your choice during this selection process becomes the foundation of your marriage. Your knowledge and ability in this area helps you to have a good marriage plan. Some people never give it that much thought and select any spouse who comes along. You would be amazed at the types of answers you get when you ask some young couples why they selected each other as mates. The more thought, factors, or strategies that you consider in this process, the more likely your potential mate will be closer to what you want—and the more likely you will have a successful marriage. Let us review these factors and strategies, especially which factors to consider in selecting a mate:

LOVE AND MARRIAGE PERSPECTIVES

A believer

If you are a Christian, your first obvious strategy will be to consider marrying a believer. It is important that both of you share the same belief in God. This can solve many problems both in the short and long term. A husband and wife can attend Sunday school, church services, and other religious activities together. In so doing, they get to know each other better. Those types of religious activities usher in love, due to spending time both with each other and with fellow worshippers. Their love for and understanding of God grows, and before they know it, the potential spouses have built a solid relationship. In other words, there is a higher correlation between long-lasting marriages in religious couples than in couples in which only one is a believer. This correlation is even higher if their religious backgrounds are similar. For example, a Baptist marries a Baptist as opposed to marrying a Catholic or a Methodist. Regardless of your church of attendance, the most important thing is for you and your future spouse to be grounded in spirituality. It's also important to note that you do not have to be a believer to have a lasting marriage. The argument here is that the more similarities you have with your potential spouse, the more likelihood that marriage will last.

Birds of a feather

The old adage about birds of a feather flocking together makes sense here. You should consider someone who is similar to you, someone who likes what you like and sees things the way that you

NUTS AND BOLTS OF SELECTING A SPOUSE

see them. For example, if you and your future wife like dressing up, you are similar in that area. If you like riding horses and your potential mate enjoys horseback riding, that is another similarity.

Let us this time imagine that you like raising hogs and your potential wife verbalizes a dislike for such an activity. In fact, you take her to your hog farm in the county for a weekend, and she complains about the stench. You shower after feeding the hogs, but she still tells you that she does not feel comfortable touching or even holding hands with you. Her reason, whether real or imagined, is that you smell like a hog, and how she feels about your stench can never be out of her system. Naturally, the entire weekend is ruined.

Compare the same scenario to one in which you meet a country girl who lives in the same city where you live. You decide to take her to your hog farm in the country for a weekend stay. As you are feeding the hogs, she jumps in and starts feeding the cows. By the time you return from the horse stables, she has also fed the chickens. She tells you that those types of activities are fun because they remind her of her adolescent days growing up on the farm. When you return to the city, she thanks you for a nice weekend and tells you that she is looking forward to returning to the farm with you someday. You do not have to be a rocket scientist to determine which of the two is similar to you, enjoying the same types of activities you do. Berschied and Reis (1998), in their study of attraction and close relationships, support the notion of similarity between partners in romantic relationships.

Attractiveness

Attraction depends on the eye of the beholder. What is attractive to Mr. A may not be attractive to Mr. Z. Certain men attribute attractiveness to a female's buttocks—specifically, how they are shaped. I have heard men comment that a particular woman has a cute butt. To some, the breasts are important. Most men dwell on the attractiveness of the face. Others perceive beauty in the tone of the skin or the length or color of the hair. Some men like women with blond hair; others like those with red or brown hair. I have also heard men talk about how crazy they are about a woman's legs, or height, or even her general appearance. There is nothing particularly wrong about each feature that you may like, for people's preferences are different. What is important is that you are sincere about what exactly you want in a woman. If you marry someone who is not the type of person you are attracted to, your eyes may eventually start wandering, since you never got what you wanted in the first place. That will not augur well for your marriage. If you marry someone you are attracted to, you increase the likelihood of your marriage lasting.

It would be a mistake to assume that women don't also have certain things that they are attracted to in the opposite sex. In the same way men are attracted to certain features, females are attracted to certain things in males. The predominant thing that seems to top the list for females is a man's chest or abdomen, with most stating that they like males with broad chests and narrow hips. Again, different people are attracted to different things.

Attraction continues to play a major role in mate selection. Several studies have looked into attractiveness in mate selection. The conclusion is that people are more often attracted to people who are similar to them than to those who are dissimilar. This is synonymous with the findings of Rosenbaum (1986), Byrne (1969), and Buss (1987).

Profession

You would be amazed how many people marry for the type of profession that the opposite sex has. When I was young, I remember being asked what I would be when I grew up. I have always stated that I would like to be a physician. A female in the neighborhood in those days was letting everybody in the neighborhood know that I would be her husband. When asked why I would be the one to marry her, her response was always, "He will be a medical doctor." I ended up not being a physician, and we lost contact after junior high school. The point of the story is that people often marry people in a particular profession. Whether marrying a person in a particular profession guarantees a good marriage is another issue, but a successful marriage depends on knowing what you want and then going after it. It could be further argued that if one marries someone in the desired profession, that person will likely do everything possible to ensure the survival of that marriage, for it is like a dream marriage for that individual.

LOVE AND MARRIAGE PERSPECTIVES

Know the person you are marrying

It is good to know and understand the person you are marrying. Dating that person will enable you to understand what makes him or her tick. Whether going to the movies, eating, or enjoying other social activities together, the objective of these activities is to grow closer and find out certain things about your potential mate. (I am not referring to sexual closeness.) This closeness will let you know, as a female, if your potential mate will open doors for you. When you go out to eat, what type of table manners will he have? Are his conversations cordial, and what type of perceptions does he have of women, family, and even his intended in-laws? How will he handle a potential angry situation? Is he explosive? How about compassionate? Is he exactly what you are looking for in a man? As a female, it is also proper to take into account that while you are observing him, he is doing the same. A female is also looking for some attributes she wants in a man, so this process of getting to know each other becomes a balanced activity.

While doing activities to get to know each other, be yourself rather than pretending to be someone else. When you are out with someone, do things as you would in your normal life. For example, conversations should be in the same tone you would normally use. Do not try to impress your potential mate, for when doing so, you are becoming who you are not. Trying to impress him or her robs a potential future spouse of knowing exactly who you are and understanding you and what you stand for.

You've probably heard people say that their husband or wife is not whom they fell in love with. You might also hear them say that he or she changed after they got married. The fact of the matter is that he or she did not change. What probably happened is that either one or both of them initially presented a false image of who they were. The other spouse locked in a wrong impression of who that person was in an attempt to impress him or her. When two people settle down in a marriage, the real people come out, sometimes prompting one to think that the other changed after marriage. That reminds me of when the marriage of Sarah Ferguson (the Duchess of York) to Prince Andrew failed. Her advice during an interview: "Know your man before marrying him." That obviously implied that she and Andrew did not know each other well prior to the marriage, thereby reiterating the importance of knowing your potential partner before marrying him or her.

No sex at that stage

Do not be too quick to jump into bed with your potential spouse prior to marriage. There are several ways of knowing a man better or knowing a woman better without rushing to have sex. Sexual intercourse between a man and a woman is a powerful thing because it involves strong feelings and emotions. Sex prior to marriage clouds the ability to think clearly and distorts the way you perceive your future spouse, because that line has been crossed. You can no longer be objective once there is sexual activity with a potential mate before knowing your intended

LOVE AND MARRIAGE PERSPECTIVES

spouse well. Sex before marriage is destructive, and my rationale for stating that is that it destroys all you have been trying to accomplish in knowing and understanding your future spouse. The quest to know him ceases, and the sexual impulse takes over. You now relate to him or her impulsively. Due to strong feelings and the rush of emotions associated with sex, you may become preoccupied with trying to satisfy your future spouse sexually. That satisfaction becomes an act and a performance issue. The problem is that with each performance, you try to outperform your previous performance. Sometimes this can be an obsession in a quest to satisfy and perform. The other danger is that the intended spouses may start looking at themselves as husband and wife and start justifying their sexual activities, saying that they are going to be married and letting things get out of hand.

Now imagine the following scenario: what if the marriage never happened after all those sexual activities? What if you are the female, and in your mind, you are honestly trying to please your intended husband with sex, and in his mind he starts thinking, *How do you know all these sexual acts? How many men have you been with?* Before you know it, your Prince Charming may start having serious doubts that you are the right woman for him. The point here is to be careful about having sex too quickly with him or her. The scriptures frown at sexual activity prior to marriage. That being said, it is not the intention of this book to tell you what to do or what not to do with your body. Still, God's intention is for sex to be enjoyed in the context of a marital relationship.

NUTS AND BOLTS OF SELECTING A SPOUSE

Age of marriage

Your age at the time of your marriage has much to do with the longevity of your marriage. The closer you were to the majority age or the emancipation age at marriage, the less likely that your marriage will last. In other words, the age of emancipation is eighteen years in most states. If you get married at the age of twenty-one or younger, which is closer to the majority or emancipation age, the more likely it is that your marriage will end in divorce. If, on the other hand, you are between the ages of twenty-two and twenty-eight years or older when you first marry, there is a stronger likelihood that your marriage will last. This is because at a younger age, the intended spouses barely understand what marriage is all about and probably lack the wherewithal and the know-how to screen or consider what is a potential good mate. The intended spouses at this age perhaps have not graduated from college or may not even have high school diplomas. There is the possibility that they do not have jobs, and even when they do, the jobs may not pay well or have proper benefits. Can you imagine being married at that age with no job, or no well-paying job? Imagine your wife having a baby when neither of you has insurance. The medical bills alone would stress the marriage. What are the chances of the marriage surviving under those conditions? Even if they were to move into the home of one of their parents, if there is no prospect of a good job, no transportation, mounting bills, and the possibility of that couple overstaying their welcome, chances of that marriage surviving are probably slim.

Now let us consider the scenario of marrying between the ages of twenty-two and twenty-eight years old. At this stage, the individuals involved can think rationally enough, probably have graduated from college, and likely have well-paying jobs. They can afford to go on dates, which will give them the opportunity to study, know, and understand each other more before making a decision to marry or not. If they decide to marry, their decision is most likely rational and not rushed. As opposed to the first scenario, where the individuals married at a much younger age, their marriage has a higher likelihood of lasting. Note that I am not stating that all marriages commenced at younger ages will fail. That was why the language was cautionary, advising about the likelihood, the probability, the degree, or the propensity. No panacea or ultimate factor or strategy is the sole determining factor or arbiter of what constitutes the absolute reality in picking out a future spouse.

Resolving differences

Marriage is the coming together of two different people. These two different individuals become one flesh. Even so, you are technically still different individuals, and there are bound to be differences. What are your plans to resolve those differences as they arise? It is always prudent to have a plan, or what I call a mechanism, to resolve differences in a marriage. Why? Physicians rehearse plans for a particular procedure, and when the need for that procedure arises, they use that plan. Firefighters have plans on how to fight a fire, and escape plans if they become overwhelmed. In marriage, it is good to have a plan to resolve differences, even rehearsing that plan in case it becomes necessary. This is so that if you get angry or any conflict arises, your spouse knows what to do—and not to escalate the situation. This will not only prolong your marriage because both of you agree on how to resolve conflict, but it can even enhance your love for one another as issues are processed.

It would be naive to think that if both of you are in love, conflict will not arise. This is a myth in marriage. There will always be differences, and the way you resolve them dictates the future of your marriage. Take into account that marriage is about feelings and emotions. A misunderstood emotion can sometimes be frustrating. The reason for this frustration is lack of a common agreement about an issue or incident. This lack of agreement is definitely a difference, and if the difference is not rectified, it can stress a marriage. That is why it is good to have plans for those unforeseen situations or circumstances. Having a resolution plan in marriage is like saving money for a rainy day. The Boy Scout motto is to be prepared, and the more prepared you are in marriage, the better likelihood of your marriage lasting.

How do you communicate with each other?

In marriage, the ability to communicate can make or break a marriage. It is a good idea when selecting a mate to consider how he or she communicates with you. Communication is what you will be doing with your intended spouse on a daily basis. You can determine a potential mate's personality by the way that he or she communicates with you. When somebody in a marriage, or a potential marriage, communicates to you as an equal, you will likely buy into what that person is saying to you. Let us assume that a potential mate talks down to you, as somebody not his or her equal. The likelihood for having a good marriage with that person appears remote. Communication is an art that can spice up a marriage.

The difference between communication and sex in marriage is that for you to have sex, you still have to communicate your intention to have sex with your spouse. So communication is everything in a marriage. The way you communicate that message can be a disaster. The reason for that is that you communicate with your whole body through verbal and nonverbal communication. The tone of your voice and the movement of your eyes, hands, neck, and even your ears in that active listening is communication. The way your intended spouse receives that communication is also part of communication. It is safe, then, to conclude that communication is a two-way street. In selecting your future spouse, listening to his or her communication languages and skills should hopefully influence your decision.

I have included a full chapter on communication in this book to illustrate its importance in marriage.

NUTS AND BOLTS OF SELECTING A SPOUSE

How long is the courtship?

There is a correlation between length of time spent on courtship and a longer, successful marriage. In other words, the longer both of you date, the more you understand each other and know your flaws, and how to relate to those flaws. A good length of time to date each other would be about two to three years. Any longer than that is unacceptable to me because the male should be able to make up his mind by that time (since the majority of proposals usually come from the males). If he does not make up his mind as to whether to propose marriage or engagement, it is a waste of the female's time. The danger in longer courtships is that the male starts getting complacent and may start taking the female for granted. There is a saying about why buy a cow if you can get the milk for free. Imagine staying in a courtship for five to six years, and at the end of the sixth year, the man tells you that he thinks things between you and him are not going to work out, and that you should stop seeing each other. You have given this man six years of your life. Are you going to sit around, probably wait another one or two years, or perhaps not? The earlier minds are made up after reasonable dating time is a good idea. On the two-year anniversary of dating, it may be proper to feel him out and see what direction he wants to take the relationship. Females have a biological clock, and that clock keeps on ticking. I have seen some men break off relationships with females they have gone with for several years, only to turn around and marry women that they have gone with less than a year. There is a difference between using somebody and dating somebody. You do not want to be used, which is why, after a certain amount of time, the man must either make his intentions known with an engagement ring or both of you should mutually agree to go in different directions and seek your futures elsewhere.

The reader may ask if the woman expecting an engagement after two years or asking the man to clarify the direction of the relationship is not an act of desperation. The answer is no. The way that I see it, no woman wants her time wasted. No man who claims to love a woman or who dates a woman should waste her time—or his own, for that matter. If you as a man do not love her enough to marry her, you should love her enough to tell her at the early stage or within that time frame. If she is not good enough for you, trust me that she is good enough for somebody else. There is another saying: one person's trash is another person's treasure.

Honesty

Another factor in selecting a mate is choosing somebody who is not going to be lying to you. Look at the fate of the women whom we discussed above regarding duration of courtship. Honesty means everything in a marriage relationship, and even in dating and courtship. The danger in lying is that once a potential mate starts lying, he will always tell another lie. Before you know it, the foundation of your relationship is a pack of lies. It's like the proverbial person in the Bible who built the foundation of his house on sand. When the rains came, it washed the sand away, and the house, including the foundation, fell. Take into account that in marriage, you share your innermost and deepest feelings. Can you imagine doing all that sharing and then finding out that all he or she has been doing is lying to you all this time? Wouldn't you feel that you have been duped or deceived? Wouldn't you feel as if your heart had been ripped out of you? That is what lies do in a marriage or in a courtship. I believe that honesty is an important criterion in selecting a potential mate, for with that honesty comes trust. When there is no trust in a real or a potential marriage, there is no relationship. A marriage with no trust is bound to fail.

Choice

This is your chance to select the woman or man of your choice. The reason I used the word "chance" is that most of the time people marry whom they think society, friends, or even colleagues would approve of, and in so doing, they sometimes miss out on the person they actually wanted—a person who could have been best for them. There are two dangers when you do not marry the person who is actually your choice. The first is missing out on what could have been your potential best relationship and love of your life, because that person could have what you were most looking for in a relationship, hence your choice. The second is that by missing out on him or her, you are letting other people make the choice for you, thereby delegating or relegating your God-given right of choice to other people. Your wife or husband is technically not yours when others make the selection

LOVE AND MARRIAGE PERSPECTIVES

process for you. It then follows that instead of living your own life, you are letting other people live your life for you and make your choices for you. You cannot stand on your own feet and still need other people's feet to stand on. People should understand that when you marry, you are marrying for yourself and not for your friends or other people. Your wife or husband will live with you, not with those other people, so why should you allow them to make decisions that will affect you and not them?

Nobody knows your potential spouse as you do. There is something about him or her that earned your affection, so you made that individual your choice. Sometimes you may not be able to explain to another person the rationale for your selection, assuming that it is even explainable, and you do not necessarily have to. You know how you feel about this person deep inside of you. Marriage is a complex emotion. Combining both is a complicated and complex process.

Colleagues can be unnecessarily intrusive. You may have to look at your colleagues' spouses and realize that you probably made a better selection than they did. Parents always want what's best for their children, but sometimes in issues like marriage, their judgment may be clouded, even when they have the best of intentions. Do not get me wrong; it is good to listen or argue with parents or colleagues in the selection of a spouse. It is wise to give their advice serious consideration. The bottom line, however, is that this is your marriage, and you have the final say.

Timing is everything

In marriage, and especially in selecting a mate, timing is everything. You may meet a potential spouse and find that he or she has everything you are looking for, or at least most of it, as no human being has everything one is looking for in a marriage. If for some reason you think that you are not ready to marry, do not proceed with the marriage. Give yourself time to review and come to terms with whatever made you to develop cold feet. In short, do not let anybody pressure you into getting married when you are not ready. I do not care what the situation or the circumstances may be. If you think that you are not ready, then you are not ready, regardless of how you slice and dice it. Always go with your gut feelings. Marriage is the decision of a lifetime. It is also a mental process. You have to be mentally and physically ready.

Commitment

Marriage is about commitment. You need someone who will be committed to stand by you in your time of need, trouble, ill health, or any other unexpected circumstances. You also need someone who can be committed to you sexually by remaining faithful and not cheating on you. In selecting a potential spouse, how he or she feels about commitment must be discussed.

Commitment is a two-way street. Both potential partners must agree on it, or the intended marriage may be a disaster before it even commences. Can you imagine finding out on your wedding day that while your wife wants to marry you, she has no intention of being committed to you and even wants fidelity omitted from the wedding vows? Such was the situation with a famous person. Pols (2009), writing an article titled "Lost at Sea" for *Time* magazine, reported how that person, on her wedding day, gave her husband and then manager an addendum to beaded to her wedding vow that stated, "I shall not hold you to any medieval code of faithfulness to me, nor shall I consider myself bound to you similarly." This illustrates the enormity of commitment in a marriage so that you and your intended spouse will be on the same page. Can you imagine the devastating effect of your wife or husband having affairs behind your back? What if you have a debilitating sickness and your spouse, who pledged to be with you in sickness or in health until death do you part, leaves you and files for a divorce? That is why it is good to discuss commitment with a potential mate. The response should give you an idea where he or she stands on such issues. That response should help you in your selection process when choosing a mate.

Commitment has obvious advantages in marriage. It enhances trust and intimacy. You and your spouse think together, as both of you have a common and shared interest. Commitment gives spouses peace of mind, knowing that they have each other to depend on in time of need.

Character

Somebody reading this book might think that I am listing too many strategies or factors for you to consider when it comes to selecting a mate. What I am attempting to do is alert people to what can help them enjoy long-lasting, meaningful, happy, and understanding marriages. Selecting a future spouse is one of your significant life decisions, if not the most significant, for your spouse will hopefully live with you and be a part of you for the rest of your life. The quality of your life depends on the decision you make, so you will want to consider all variables in order to make the right decision. You do not want your marriage to fail before it even commences or as it is commencing.

A person's character is ingrained at a certain age. Once that happens, that person's character becomes part of his or her constitutional makeup. In other words, as you select your future spouse, consider his or her character. You may want to take into account how that individual relates to the following: you, his or her parents, potential in-laws, children in general, anger, frustration tolerance, commitment, and things like that. Ask yourself if you can trust and depend on this individual. It does not take rocket science to figure out the imperativeness of trust and dependability in a relationship. Look at it this way: in racing, horses are good, but I'd rather have a mule that I can trust and depend on than a horse that I can't count on. That is how character is in marriage—you should have an ally and confidante in whom you have absolute trust.

LOVE AND MARRIAGE PERSPECTIVES

Ambition and drive

If aspiring couples have a compatible amount of ambition, it illustrates some similarities and the potential of that marriage lasting if consummated. Having the same or comparable levels of ambition tends to be a good match in marriage. Imagine this scenario. One of the intended spouses has high ambition and drive. He or she had aspirations of being a pharmacist. Within four years of their dating, one finished college and became a registered pharmacist. The other has less drive, works off and on, and never even completed college. If they marry, what do you think will be the direction of that marriage?

A couple of years ago, I was watching a TV program called *Cheaters*. This program goes undercover to catch cheating spouses and the intended couple on camera. I saw an extremely attractive woman on this program. She was in college studying for a Bachelor of Science degree in nursing (BSN). The cheating fiancé was not in college and had low ambition and drive. He could not even keep his job as a warehouse clerk. You could tell that she was madly in love with him from her actions and how she verbalized her love for him. *Cheater always does* an update to their stories. I was fortunate to catch the update story on her during the follow-up program. She had her BSN degree then and was working at a hospital in the city where she was residing. She'd also enrolled as a part-time student for a master's degree in public health (MPH) and was dating a gynecologist in private practice. She was asked about her former fiancé, the warehouse clerk. To paraphrase her response, she stated that she wished him well, but that he lacked the drive and ambition to compete in today's world. She'd tried to pull him up but had to let go when it became obvious that he was not likely to change. The female he was cheating with had no job, was not in college, and had very low self-esteem.

Unrealistic expectations

People enter into marriage for different reasons. We've heard of females who want to marry a rich man, and I met a woman with that type of mentality. I asked her what made her think that she could marry a rich man. She stated that there are rich old men looking for sexy females like her. She would do whatever she could do to get a rich old man to marry her. She talked about giving him sex and more sex until he got confused. We discussed how sex should be enjoyed in the context of a marital relationship, not designed to trap a man in marriage. Her response was that all that scripture was none of her business.

My point is that you have to be careful whom you select as your spouse because people come into marriage with ulterior motives, and both of you may end up having different expectations. We are cautioned in the Bible to be careful of wolves in sheep's clothing. Sometimes when people professes love it may not necessarily be true, so we have to be careful about whom we marry, for some people come into marriage with different expectations than we do.

LOVE AND MARRIAGE PERSPECTIVES

Marriage is joy. Marriage is happiness. But it can also be a disaster if your spouse has unrealistic expectations or has different opinions about marriage than you do. It is always a good practice to talk things out before marriage rather than assuming that you and your intended spouse are on the same page. Sometimes one may discover what appears to be an unrealistic expectation but chooses to ignore it, thinking that with time, things will get better. The irony is that things can get worse sometimes, which could be prevented if things were ironed out before marriage. Remember what we discussed previously—about a person's character in regard to his constitutional makeup. Once a person's DNA is institutionalized, it is difficult to change that person. While discussing marital expectations with your potential spouse, if the issue in question is something that you cannot live with, you will want to reconsider your choice of mate or your plans.

Behavioral problems

While discussing other factors, we have touched on some other issues concerning behavior. This particular behavior focuses on substance abuse. If your spouse-to-be is abusing alcohol or other addictive substances, it is best that he or she get help prior to marriage. It is also imperative for the spouse not abusing the substance to understand the dynamics of addiction in case of a potential relapse. I have worked in addiction counseling for many years, and believe me; I have seen substance abuse issues ruin marriages. The reason why a potential spouse should consider this as a selecting criterion is that there is no miracle cure. In addiction, all one can do is to be aware of the situation, manage his or her impulses, and avoid people, places, or things that can trigger relapse. I have seen people relapse after years of abstinence. I am not saying that the relapse is due to marriage. All I am stating is that there is always a likelihood that one can relapse, and the other spouse should have a mechanism in place in case that happens. If you think that as a potential spouse, you may not be able to cope with that, then it is up to you to rethink your choice of your potential mate.

Money management

Finance is a major source of marital discord. Marriages have been ruined because couples cannot agree on money matters. It is therefore imperative that prior to marriage, potential couples should discuss money matters. This includes who makes the major decisions about money. Issues relating to money are usually done as a team. Sometimes one spouse's opinion may outweigh the other's. Discussion should be exhaustive about investment portfolios, 401(k)s, and other investment options.

Conclusions

It is pertinent to note that the personalities of the two people in a marriage comprise one of the most important factors. Kelly et al. (2003, 446) noted the following: "It is clearly important to realize that personalities of the individuals involved in a relationship are important determinants of the interaction process that takes place in that relationship. However, just as

LOVE AND MARRIAGE PERSPECTIVES

personalities influence relationships, so many relationships influence the personality process."

By the same reasoning, regarding personality development, Caspi and Herbener (1990) wrote: "Situation selection is relevant to the understanding of not only relationship development and process, but also personality development (continuity and change) in the context of relationships."

The degree of love and what both spouses intend to accomplish in marriage are other determining factors. One can consider all these strategies in selecting a spouse, and there may still be some problems down the road in marriage. Who is to say that there is not going to be a problem in a marriage? What these factors or strategies will do is lessen the incidence of the problems, or at least bring them to a manageable level. The key to a problem in marriage is how it is managed or resolved. Not that people want problems in a marriage, but some problems even strengthen marriage if resolved timely, amicably, and appropriately. Regardless of the books that you read, or do not read, regarding mate selection, it is for you and your spouse to make your marriage joyful and happy so you can live happily ever after.

Love is a fruit in season at all times, and within the reach of every hand.

—Mother Teresa of Calcutta

CHAPTER TWO

Being In Love, Staying In Love, And Growing In Love

Love begins when a person feels another person's needs to be as important as his own.

—Sullivan

IMAGINE THE RUSH of feelings when someone you care for tells you "I love you." My own feelings and emotions are still vivid in my mind from the first time someone other than family told me that. This was several years ago. Frankly, I was not even mature enough to understand what love was, as I understand it now, but it sure made me feel good—not only because it was the first time I heard those three words, but because I sincerely cared -- or thought that I cared -- for this individual. If you take yourself back to your first love, you probably still remember having the same emotions.

Attributes of love

Attributes of love encompass closeness, warmth, acceptance, pleasure, and security. Let's explore each one.

LOVE AND MARRIAGE PERSPECTIVES

Closeness

Love gives a feeling of closeness with the one you love. This feeling is profound and sometimes indescribable. The closer you feel to the one you love, the more meaning you derive from being in love. Closeness helps you bond with your love, and because of that closeness, you can do things for the one you love.

Warmth

There is a feeling of warmth toward the one you love. This warmth actually starts from inside of you and then transfers to your lover. When this warmth is reciprocated, you and the one you love feel great affection toward each other. You open up your heart to him or her. A flood of emotions goes with opening up yourself and your heart to this individual. This can be damaging if it is not done in the context of a marital relationship. Caution is warranted here if you do not know this individual well, or if that warmth is one-sided. It is always a good practice to look deep before you leap, for if you do not, you may land on a hard object.

Acceptance

I still remember a song by Teddy Pendergrass which, when paraphrased, goes something like this: *It's so good, so good, when somebody loves you back.* Somebody loving you back shows acceptance and mutual feelings. It further denotes and shows appreciation, understanding, and respect for each other. When love is on equal footing and the attributes stated herein are injected into that love, it will be an extraordinary relationship. If all these attributes are present and the feelings are mutual in the marital relationship, that marriage has a strong chance of lasting. There are respect, acceptance, love, understanding, and appreciation, which mean your marriage is on equal footing. You may ask whether those attributes aren't automatically inherent in a marriage. You would be amazed at some of the reasons that people marry—and not all do so because of love. Some marry for other ulterior motives that are beyond the scope of this book.

Pleasure

People derive pleasure from love. When people are in love, especially a good love relationship, it brings happiness as long as the two people involved in the relationship work hard to make it happy. Under the principle of utilitarianism, people seek pleasure—looking for what makes them happy. They move away from pain while seeking happiness. Now can you see why so many people want to be in love or are in love or growing in love and staying in love? Frankly, I have yet to find someone who does not want to be loved or does not want to love somebody. Love has built-in pleasure as an added fringe benefit, if that loving relationship is in the context of a marriage. The issue here is that certain people want the benefits of marriage without being married. Do not get me wrong; there is nothing wrong with being in love. The concern is that sharing at the very deepest levels, like sexual intimacy, should fall within the scope of a marital relationship. A great

LOVE AND MARRIAGE PERSPECTIVES

debate continues to rage in this area. This book is not about condemning or disagreeing with anybody's view on sexual intimacy.

Security

Love is security. It could mean being secure in your mind, knowing that your spouse loves you. It could also mean being secure in his or her arms while cuddling. Further, it could also mean financial security, knowing that you are financially being taken care of. Remember that I previously stated in this section that people marry for different reasons. Financial security is one of those. Some people marry because the other person has money. They may develop love for that individual in the process of the security that his or her money provides in the marriage. It is still an open question whether the love that individual develops is for the love of money – or in other words, whether they love that spouse for who they are, or for what they can get out of that spouse.

The word love

There are so many uses of the word love that sometimes the love or the type of love that you are talking about or trying to project is lost in the meaning. Let us look at some examples of sentences with the word love and try to decipher the type of love being talked about. *I love my mother. Of course, I love my grandmother, and I love my daddy too. I'm in love with my red car. Boy, I love my flat-screen TV. I love my woman. I love my dog. I love traveling, especially to Europe. I love to learn French. I love that movie. I love*

BEING IN LOVE, STAYING IN LOVE, AND GROWING IN LOVE

sex, of course; there is no doubt about that one. I am in love with my blue jeans. In this regard, Lepine (1999, 149) noted: "We talk casually about loving everything from golf to a particular brand of hot dogs, and in the process, our understanding of what real love is has been cheapened beyond recognition."

Our culture seems obsessed with love, but what type of love are we talking about here? Turn on the TV for about fifteen minutes. Every minute, flip to a different channel with your remote control; you may be surprised to note that out of fifteen channels you will watch in those fifteen minutes, an average of twelve of the channels have some type of subtle or obvious message of love being disseminated. This is my own experience. It may not be the same for someone else. Consider the commercials on TV; sex and love are being used to sell products. Tune in to any music radio station of your choice, whether it plays hip-hop, jazz, country and western, soul, rhythm and blues, and you will notice that 70 to 80 percent are love songs. Turn back to your TV and watch some music videos. What will behold your eyes will likely be the raunchiest of sexual performances, making you wonder how it got on TV in the first place. Our society has become obsessed with love and sex. In the midst of all this, let us attempt to define what love is.

Definition of love

Good luck trying to define love, for it means different things to different people. The definition of love depends on from whose perspective you are trying or attempting to define love. There is sexual love; there is romantic love; there is Christian love; there is conditional and unconditional love.

The key words and phrases in defining love often include the following: benevolence, concern, deep attraction, strong affection, rush of passion, pleasure, happiness, desire, warm attachment, caresses, devotion, loyalty to one another, tenderness, caring and sharing, lust, cherishing, commitment, unselfishness, and a host of others. Random House Webster's Dictionary (2001, 427) defines love in this way: "A profoundly tender, passionate affection for another person, an intense personal attachment or affection; a person toward whom love is felt and a strong enthusiasm of liking."

Stages of romantic love

Romantic love is a good feeling if we genuinely and sincerely have someone who loves us romantically. It is a better feeling if that person is your spouse and you can reciprocate what that person feels for you. This normally begins when we see somebody who catches our attention; we perceive that person as being beautiful or handsome. Remember that beauty is in the eye of the beholder, in that people have their own criteria of beauty or handsomeness. To some, it could be a woman with a certain type of shape and body features. To some, it could be a male with features that they perceive as manly. At this stage, no one has considered what is on the inside of the person. We tend to be captivated by outward characteristics. People tend to forget at that stage that not all that glitters is gold—and that there is more than physical beauty. As we start talking to that person, the stages of love may start to develop. Let us now review the stages of romantic love.

The talking stage

As the name connotes, we are interested in talking to a person who has caught our eye. We try to convince this person that he or she is the best thing that ever happened to us. Telephone numbers are probably exchanged at this time. If the talk continues to progress favorably, it starts leading to the next stage of romantic relationships, which is the wooing stage.

The wooing stage

At this stage, the wooer, often the male, will start asking her to go out to eat or to enjoy other activities. The wooer wants to be on his best behavior, with the intention of impressing the person he is wooing. This gives the female the chance to watch the mannerisms of the individual. It gives her the opportunity to observe if the man opens doors, lets her be seated first, takes her coat or jacket, or anything else that piques her interest and imagination.

Irrational stage

As things start progressing, both of them, assuming that they continue to attract each other, often start having mutual thoughts of being together or exclusive. If there are no distractions from other partners, like an ex-boyfriend or ex-girlfriend, and they focus on each other, they might progress to the next stage, all things being equal. This stage is known as the irrational stage because of the emotions associated with exclusivity, especially with distractions from ex-friends.

Going steady

At this stage, they definitely become an item, and as the name of this stage implies, they are going steady or being exclusive. They cannot seem to get enough of each other. Where you see one, you see the other. In some cases, this may lead to obsession; being together becomes the dominant theme in their lives. Depending on their personalities and adjustment, nothing else matters to them. For the reason stated above, some people refer to the going steady stage as the obsessive stage. Some at this stage progress and go on to the next stage, which is called the proposal or engagement stage. Some may fall by the wayside because of factors like cheating, objections from family, and so on. This is called the dip or pit stage.

Dip or pit stage

This is known as the dip stage because the relationship has plunged. It is also known as the pit stage because the relationship has fallen into a pit. Depending on the causative factor that necessitated the relationship plunging or falling, it may still be resurrected to the next stage—the proposal or engagement stage. Unresurrected relationships end up dying a natural death at this stage.

The proposal or engagement stage

This is when two people decide that they are taking their relationship to the finish line and announce their engagement. The battle is not over until they say "I do." I have seen many a couple make it to the engagement level, but marriage still eludes them because of some issues they could not reconcile.

Spiritual love

According to Strong (2001), the word love is used 310 times in the Bible. The mention of love in Biblical literature is profound, its meaning undoubtedly clear. Let us explore the following:

> *Love suffers long and is kind; love does not envy; love does not parade itself, is not puffed up; does not behave rudely, does not seek its own, is not provoked, thinks no evil; does not rejoice in iniquity, but rejoices in the truth; bears all things, believes all things, hopes all things, endures all things.* (I Corinthians 13:4–7)

The foregoing illustrates the powerfulness and awesomeness of spiritual love. It is the absolute totality of every aspect of life, everything and anything that you can think of. Analyze this sentence and you may start noticing more the impact and implications of spiritual love. Love "bears all things, believes all things, hopes all things, and endures all things." This is as clear and as absolute as it gets. The word love as used above speaks for itself, and the words speak for themselves. It clarifies what love is and what love is not.

The need to love one another

I always ponder the waste of love and time when I see spouses arguing and fighting over trivial things, when they are always in disagreement instead of loving each other. Couples should be enjoying love, not fighting. The Bible admonishes us to love one another:

> *Beloved, let us love one another, for love is of God; and everyone who loves is born of God and knows God. He who does not love does not know God, for God is love. In this the love of God was manifested toward us, that God has sent His only begotten Son into the world, that we might live through Him. In this is love, not that we loved God, but that He loved us and sent His Son to be the propitiation for our sins. Beloved, if God so loved us, we also ought to love one another.* (I John 4:7–11)

Can you imagine the great price paid for us to be in love because God gave up his only begotten son for us? All we have to do is love one another as God loved us.

BEING IN LOVE, STAYING IN LOVE, AND GROWING IN LOVE

The perfect love

Love between spouses is not perfect. In this world that we live in, nothing is perfect, including love, but we can strive and do the best that we can under the circumstances. In spiritual love, perfection is a different issue, as illustrated in the First Epistle of John.

> *Love has been perfected among us in this: that we may have boldness in the Day of Judgment; because as He is, so are we in this world. There is no fear in love; but perfect love casts out fear, because fear involves torment. But he who fears has not been made perfect in love. We love Him because He first loved us* (I John 4:17–19).

Loving without hypocrisy

If you love your spouse, show that you love him or her. Focus and concentrate your attention on your spouse. There is exclusivity in marriage. If you start cheating on your spouse, not only are you no longer exclusive, but you love with hypocrisy. Love comes in all shapes, all sizes, all colors, and once you make up your mind to love someone, mean it and let there be no hypocrisy about it. This is evident in the Epistles of Paul the Apostle to the Romans, where he states as follows:

> *Let love be without hypocrisy. Abhor what is evil. Cling to what is good. Be kindly affectionate to one another with*

> *brotherly love, in honor giving preference to one another; not lagging in diligence, fervent in spirit, serving the Lord; rejoicing in hope, patient in tribulation, continuing steadfastly in prayer; distributing to the needs of the saints given to hospitality.* (Romans 12:9–13)

God's love

In the scripture, it is mentioned numerous times that God loves us. For the purpose of this chapter, I will mention only two. What is the significance of God's love in a marital relationship? The significance is that God loves us, and as followers of Christ, we should walk and strive to live life as Christ did. God's love is total. God's love is eternal. God's love is perpetual. God loves us without ceasing. Concomitant to that argument is being Christ like; having his qualities and practicing his teachings, we are supposed to love our spouses the same way we love ourselves. The scripture said in the Epistle of Paul the Apostle to the Romans:

> *But God demonstrates His own love toward us, in that while we were still sinners, Christ died for us.* (Romans 5:8).

> *Being Christ like gives us access to faith—but we also glory in tribulations, knowing that tribulation produces perseverance; and perseverance, character; and character, hope.* (Romans 5:3–4)

We need these attributes in marriage. A marriage that has a

mechanism for tribulations, that possesses character, perseverance, and hope, has a greater propensity for vitality and survival as compared to a marriage that does not have those. The Apostle Paul noted:

> *Yet in all these things we are more than conquerors through Him who loved us. For I am persuaded that neither death nor life, nor angels nor principalities nor powers, nor things present nor things to come, nor height nor depth, nor any other created thing, shall be able to separate us from the love of God which is in Christ Jesus our Lord.* (Romans 8:37–39)

The same way that nothing separates us from the love of God, we are being challenged that we should let nothing separate us from our spouses and our marriages.

Sincere love

It is pertinent to close this section by discussing sincere love, in that with sincerity in our marriages and when dealing with others, things have a definite and reflective meaning. More attributes of love and marriage necessitate concluding as follows:

> *But in all things we commend ourselves as ministers of God: in much patience, in tribulations, in needs, in distresses, in stripes, in imprisonments, in tumults, in labors, in sleeplessness, in fastings; by purity, by knowledge, by longsuffering ...*

> *by the power of God, by the armor of righteousness on the right hand and on the left, by honor and dishonor, by evil report and good report; as deceivers, and yet true; as unknown, and yet well known; as dying and behold we live; as chastened, and yet not killed; as sorrowful, yet always rejoicing; as poor, yet making many rich; as having nothing, and yet possessing all things.* (2 Corinthians 6:4–10)

The above is a totality of factors needed in marital relationships. If we have more of these factors in a marriage, the more stable and meaningful that marriage should be.

What spiritual love is not?

I remember when I was in junior high school, and the teacher of one of my classes was teaching about words and their opposites. She had two columns on the blackboard. One column had words with certain meanings; for example, "good" was written in one column. The opposite column had nothing in it. We were to discuss it for a few minutes and then come up with what we thought was the opposite. One of my group members said that the opposite of any word is what that word is not, but he wouldn't come up with a specific word that denoted the opposite of the word being discussed. What spiritual love is not, is the opposite of spiritual love.

If you are looking for a spouse, it is best to find one who is grounded in spiritual love. There are other attributes of other types of love, including romantic love, which are important to consider. A spouse with balanced attributes seems more sensible, but the choice ultimately rests between you and your partner or future partner. If you are unmarried and looking for a spouse, keep in mind that if something looks too good, it probably is. On the other hand, what is bad is bad, regardless of how you look at it. Bear that in mind as you select your spouse. The Second Epistle of Paul the Apostle to Timothy states:

> *For men will be lovers of themselves, lovers of money, boasters, proud, blasphemers, disobedient to parents, unthankful, unholy, unloving, unforgiving, slanderers, without self-control, brutal, despisers of good, traitors, headstrong, haughty, lovers of pleasure rather than lovers of God, having a form of godliness but denying its power. And from such people turn away.* (2 Timothy 3:2–5)

Significance of faith in love and marriage

According to Strong (2001, 373–75), the Bible mentioned "words associated with faith" 19 times. "Faith" was mentioned 246 times, "faithful" 86 times, and "faithfully" 8 times. Faith or words associated with it were mentioned 359 times in the Bible. Faith is defined in the Bible as "the substance of things hoped for, the evidence of things not seen" (Hebrews 11:1). Random House Webster's Dictionary (2001, 254) defined faith as "confidence or trust in a person or thing, belief in God; a system of religious beliefs."

Faith is a Christian belief. It is one of the cardinal doctrines in which Christians feel a strong connection to God. The more grounded one is in his or her faith, the stronger the attachment that person is to his or her faith. Faith is good for marriage in that it is futuristic. By this, I mean that it gives hope that things will be okay, thereby giving couples hope and something to look for in the marriage. This hope is incumbent on the couples working hard to achieve that objective. This could be working to resolve issues that are threatening their marriage, or making things better in their marriage. Being prayerful is another way of working through issues in marriage. Prayer in marriage has a dual purpose. First, it helps when working through issues. Second, it further helps in uniting couples as they seek a common goal through prayer. A couple tends to bond more, and marriage is further solidified because of it. Let us review briefly some articles of faith in the Bible.

Articles of faith

There are several articles of faith in Biblical literature. A few will be mentioned or addressed here to help in reiterating the importance of faith.

Crossing the Red Sea: Can you imagine the Red Sea parting as Israelites passed through? The Red Sea became a dry land for them, while the Egyptians attempting the same thing were drowned. The same chill and rush of emotions that I experienced watching the movie *The Ten Commandments* came back as I was writing this particular section. What an act of faith.

Abraham offering of Isaac: Abraham's faith was tested when he was about to offer his son Isaac for sacrifice, but God sent a ram instead.

Noah's ark: It was by faith that Noah prepared an ark, thereby saving his household.

As stated above, there are several mentions of faith and acts of faith in Biblical literature, as review of that literature attests. Three acts of faith were mentioned only for illustrative purposes, to remind us that we should do the following:

> *Run with endurance the race that is set before us, looking unto Jesus, the author and finisher of our faith, who for the joy that was set before Him endured the cross, despising the same, and has sat down at the right had of the throne of God.* (Hebrews 12:1–2)

Marriage is endurance and perseverance. It is also a race, but the direction of the race depends on the people in that marriage.

Impact and implications

There are obvious subtle implications and messages as you read about spiritual love and messages that undoubtedly impact our marriage. Let us review them:

From Biblical readings, we have seen the impact of faith in our belief system. Imagine something or somebody that even the sea will obey. God made the Red Sea part for his people to walk through. The ones not designated by him perished in the sea. It is with faith that the sea was parted. It is also said that faith can move mountains. When you believe in God, you do so by faith. If we follow the definition of faith, we have not seen God, at least not in plain view, but we believe in God. If I entrust myself to God, I should entrust my marriage to God through prayers. With those prayers, I am asking God for guidance and direction in my marriage. The fact that I asked God for favors of marriage in my prayers does not mean that I should cease making other efforts in improving my marriage. I still have to control my anger, work on my interpersonal skills, avoid cheating on my wife, help my wife with household chores, and a gamut of other issues.

Spiritual love is patience, and a love that endures all things. Let me not quote but paraphrase the definition of the word "all," as in Webster's Dictionary, to illustrate love as well as its impact on and implications in marriage. "All is the whole of; the greatest possible; beyond all doubt; everything; completely; everything considered; in the slightest degree; for any reason; in any way, all in all and in any way." The Bible states, "Love never fails." In a comparative analysis, mention was made of faith, hope, and love, "but the greatest of these is love." The impact and implications of that is that with unconditional love -- as opposed to conditional love -- you and your spouse can surmount any marital problem if both of you sincerely want to resolve the problem. Unconditional love is spiritual. Conditional love is loving someone contingent

BEING IN LOVE, STAYING IN LOVE, AND GROWING IN LOVE

on what you get from that person, or vice versa. If someone loves you in this manner and the thing that he or she derives from you or the relationship evaporates, the love is no longer there. That derivation can be sex, gifts, or whatever. Therefore, in unconditional marriage, love reigns supreme, for somebody loves you for who you are, not what he or she can get out of you. Unconditional love is loving others the way they are.

We were admonished to love one another, in that God is love, and as God loves us, so shall we love one another. As God loves us, so shall we love our spouses? In marriage, we become one body with our spouses. We all love ourselves, so since we are each one body and nobody hates himself, it follows that we love, not hate, our spouses. By virtue of that "one body," we love our spouses the same way we love ourselves. Love has been perfected among us spiritually, and with that perfection, there is no fear in love. This explains why unconditional love has no record of wrongdoings, and why it is total and complete. It's because we love boldly, with no fear. Can you imagine your spouse loving you fearlessly? Some people also know this as loving unselfishly. Can you imagine the impact and the rush of the emotions, trust, and understanding with that type of love?

Hypocritical love is dangerous because the hypocritical lover is a façade. It is sometimes initially difficult to identify or detect the hypocritical lover. With time, the hypocritical lover manifests itself. The one being loved hypocritically may already have attachment issues at the time of discovery. A hypocritical lover

LOVE AND MARRIAGE PERSPECTIVES

is like a wolf in sheep's clothing, and that is why it is important to know your intended spouse at the beginning of the selection process, before saying "I do."

In spiritual love, nothing separates us from the love of God, which manifested in Jesus Christ our Lord. The profound impact and implications of that is that in marriage, we are glued to our spouse. We do not want to be separated from God because of our belief in God. Similarly, we should not be separated from our spouses and should try to work out issues that confront our marriages. Take into account that in Malachi, one sentence is profound: "God hates divorce."

The only person who can make or break your marriage is you. Someone may ask, "What if my spouse makes me angry or is the cause of the problem in our marriage?" The response is that every coin has two sides. In your mind, you may think that your spouse is the cause. Have you pondered what your spouse thinks is the cause of the problems? The fact is that blaming or pointing accusing fingers at each other will not solve the problem. Each has to take responsibility, and the type or the amount of responsibility taken determines the vitality of the marriage. The foregoing further goes back to show that you are responsible in your own marriage, and you can make or break it. So what you do or do not do is the key. I refer you to the Epistle of James on that subject, to show that what you do or don't do counts:

> *But be doers of the word, and not hearers only, deceiving yourselves. For if anyone is a hearer of the word and not a doer, he is like a man observing his natural face in a mirror; for he observes himself, goes away, and immediately forgets what kind of man he was.* (James 1:22–24)

Loving and being in love—some clarification

This chapter would not be complete if I did not discuss the "BSG" of love. By that, I mean *B* for being in love, *S* for staying in love, and *G* for growing in love. I will clarify some misconceptions about love and my own naivete before my studies in this area. I used to think there was only one type of intimacy, and you guessed it: sexual intimacy. I once liked a woman and was thinking seriously about dating her. If things turned out right, she might have been a serious candidate for marriage. I asked a colleague of mine his impression about her. His response: "We are intimate." He and the person I admired were in an intimate sexual relationship. That nixed the idea of being with her. Let us attempt to identify types of intimacy.

Physical

Physical intimacy is what I have discussed above. Some know it as sexual intimacy. It includes caring, touching, affectionate embraces, and hugs. It further consists of tender words and, of course, passionate union, which is a euphemism for sexual intercourse.

Emotional

Emotional intimacy has to do with both spouses being friends before marriage and friends in the marriage. The deeper the friendship, the deeper their bonding becomes. It further encompasses other things, such as sharing dreams, hopes, and aspirations, and offers freedom to express emotions and develop common and mutual interests in marriage.

Spiritual

Spiritual intimacy has to do with your spirituality, such as a couple praying together. They are unified in their church activities and other devotional areas pertaining to their spiritual bonding. Take into account the saying that the family that prays together stays together—and imagine what praying can do for your marriage.

Dimensions in intimacy

One may tend to ask which aspect of intimacy is needed most in a marriage. To me, each of these intimacies complements the other, and none is exclusive of the others. All three should work together and go hand in hand. Man is a three-dimensional being. The soul, spirit, and body are technically one, and physical, emotional, and spiritual intimacy together yield oneness. This approach is sometimes called the holistic approach because of this union or oneness. Some therapies using the holistic approach or theory consider one's total physical and psychological state in the etiology and treatment. Remember that God made us three-dimensional, and those three mentioned intimacies together equal oneness. Sex alone without the other two intimacies not only doesn't complete marriage, but doesn't complement it either. So a balanced approach to intimacy in marriage is the combination or the unification of the three -- hence holistic or dimensional. Having cleared up some misconceptions about intimacy, I will now clarify some misconceptions about love.

Sexual appeasement

I still remember a song that goes like this: *I am not a simple girl. I am not the type of girl you can lay down and think that everything is okay. No, no, no, I am not.* I do not know the artist of the song, but when that song came out, it was always played on an FM radio station called Magic 102. The reason for this story is that it exactly explains or illustrates this sex appeasement misconception. Some couple thinks that regardless of the problem they have in their marriage, the problem is solved once they have sex. This is not so. You may feel good having sex, but that does not mean the problem is gone. The problem does not go away until you resolve it.

It never fails: some couples have arguments and then tell you they made up. When you ask how, the answer is that they made up by having sex, thus using sex to fulfill their emotional needs. Can you imagine the type of argument or further misunderstanding that will happen with spouses that use this technique as a mechanism for resolving issues? One refuses to have sex after an argument because his or her feelings are still hurt. The partner that is refused sex may boil into a rage because the other spouse denied sex to him or her. Now both have an added problem, including the original issue, to resolve. One spouse may start seeing himself or herself as the other's sex object, especially if the spouse that always precipitates the problem is the one being refused makeup sex. This sexual appeasement approach is sometimes known as the lying down syndrome because the couple uses sex (lying down) as a mechanism for resolving issues.

Not expressing your thoughts

Some couples think that being in love comes with mind reading. Your rationale might be that if your spouse loves you, he or she should be able to know what you think. Marriage is a close union of a man and a woman, not a mind reading exercise. If you do not talk about your needs, they will not be met. So clarity is important in marriage. Assumptions will only send conflicting and misunderstood messages.

Understanding grows with time

Some people tend to assume that the more or longer they stay together in a relationship, the closer understanding they should have. This is not necessarily true. How about people whose marriages disintegrate after several years of marriage? The two people in the marriage must foster closeness or understanding. A number of factors come into play, including their chemistry and personalities.

Action and reaction

Your action in your marriage determines the trend, direction, and duration of your marriage. The way you treat your spouse determines his or her reaction to you. I remember being advised by an older person to always treat my woman right. Be nice to her, for what you put into your relationship is what you will get in return. If you open doors for your woman, she will open her heart for you. Behavior counts in love. Yes, there is a strong correlation between behavior and marriage outcome. The next time your spouse starts acting unfavorably toward you, you may want to look inward to yourself. It may not be her; it could be you. Marriage requires and warrants good behavior.

Deciding to love

Love is a decision. It is true that people fall in love, but it is our decision to do so. You may have heard the saying "I was swept off my feet." That may be true, but you are the one who allowed it. Allowing it is a decision you made. If you did not want to be swept off your feet, it would not have happened. So it is a misconception that people fall in love; rather, people decide to be in love. People decide to stay in love. People decide to grow in love. People decide to get married. Unfortunately, people also decide to end their marriages. Keep in mind that any relationship can be valid to the extent we work toward it. The direction of the relationship depends not only on that hard work, but on the collective experience of both spouses who have learned in the course of that relationship. This demonstrates that while personalities influence the success or failure of marriages, decisions do as well. Love definitely is a decision. Why? The reason is that it involves feelings and emotions of the individuals in that relationship.

Maintaining passion throughout marriage

It is a misconception that being in love or being married automatically comes with passion. It is also a misconception that once that passion is in the marriage, it stays forever. Passion is a necessary ingredient in a marital relationship. It spices up marriage. Personally, I call passion and sex the fringe benefits of marriage. Some spouses tend to forget sometimes that at some point in the marriage relationship, passion may fade. Many variables account for diminishing passion in a marriage. Some include lack of interest, sickness, old age, past experiences, possibly childhood abuse, medication side effects, erectile dysfunction, cheating, and so on and so forth. Depending on the precipitating or even the predisposing causative factors of diminishing passion, the question is, can marriage endure without passion? This is where the personalities of the people in the marriage come into play. The original intention of their marriage also comes in, as people marry for various reasons. You may have already noticed that not all marriages are necessarily for romantic reasons. I still remember a few words and phrases during my study of Latin. *Amor vincit omnia* translates to "love conquers all." You would be amazed what the power of love can do or conquer in those instances.

Disclosure

Disclosure enhances the flow of marriage. It is helpful in resolving marital conflicts, especially where sexual indiscretion may have happened and trust is low. It may sometimes have its drawbacks. Before I get into what may be probable drawbacks, it is pertinent to state that I cannot imagine a reason or a situation for one spouse to harbor a secret or not want to share all his or her thoughts and feelings in a marriage. Once one or both spouses start withholding issues in a marriage by not sharing completely, that becomes the beginning of a structural defect in that marriage. A marriage should be developed to the point where there is absolute trust and confidence in each other. For this trust to continue, a mechanism has to be in place to avoid whatever would arouse legitimate suspicion. That being said, the question arises: should one disclose everything in a marriage? There are two schools of thought in this area. Let's review them.

The first school of thought

The first school of thought takes the view that everything should

LOVE AND MARRIAGE PERSPECTIVES

be disclosed in a marriage. The rationale behind that line of thought is that you are robbing your mate of intimacy by withholding some issues or avoiding full disclosure. They view it as cheating your spouse out of information that he or she is entitled to have. Take into consideration that both of you are now one, and not disclosing fully is probably not in the best interest of the marriage.

A further argument: if your spouse were to withhold from you, how would you feel? So put yourself in your spouse's shoes by being empathetic and disclosing issues that your spouse is entitled to know about. "Entitled to," by this school of thought, means everything should be disclosed. Technically, entitlement may mean or could be interpreted as what the withholding spouse thinks that he or she should disclose, thereby avoiding total disclosure of derogatory information. This school looks at marriage as immersing yourself, your feelings, and your emotions entirely; and if you withhold or don't disclose fully, the marriage or its emotions are no longer complete. The final argument is that there are no part-time marriages, and the rules of marriage are universal. Not fully disclosing is like a part-time marriage, making you seem as if you are making up your marriage rules for your own convenience—and as they suit you. What then becomes of the marriage if your spouse starts making his or her own rules instead of following the accepted universal rules of marriage?

The second school of thought

The second school of thought is of the opinion that you can disclose some information, but that it is not a good idea to disclose fully. The rationale is that you do not want to disclose what will hurt the feelings of your spouse and possibly mean the demise of your marriage. An appendix to those two arguments is as follows: does not fully disclosing what you think will hurt your spouse give you an excuse and a license to do as you please under the pretense of not wanting to hurt the other spouse? If that is the case, when does the offending behavior stop? Should it continue forever? How about repentance?

As for the other line of argument in not wanting to ruin the marriage, shouldn't the offending spouse think about his or her behavior on the marriage before acting? How about taking responsibility for behavior or actions? Let us say, for example, that a wife has an affair. Should she go tell her husband, "Honey, I had an affair. Can you please forgive me?" Should she keep quiet since the husband is unaware of it? Assuming the husband finds out and confronts the wife, the wife may ask for forgiveness, and the husband may make that forgiveness contingent on full disclosure. Should the wife just admit the affair and apologize profusely? Further, should the wife hurt the husband's feelings by disclosing all the details of the affair by telling the husband the name of the guy, the place, how many times the affair occurred, the sexual positions involved, and other grueling details? This school advocates disclosure enough to accept the affair, apologize, and hope your spouse can forgive you so you can move on with the marriage.

Full disclosure is a hot issue in marriage. The personalities of the people in the marriage and their propensity to forgive, as well as their disposition on love, are most likely the determining factors here. Speaking of the propensity to forgive, it is now appropriate to explore forgiveness in relation to marriage and love.

Propensity to forgive and logic of forgiveness

Forgiveness is giving the person that hurts you a gift. This definition will undoubtedly confuse someone new to forgiveness. Why is it a gift? Why are you giving someone who hurt you a gift? Is that gift to thank him or her for hurting you? Sometimes the explanation and rationale behind the logic of forgiveness is irrational and difficult to explain and even to understand. In forgiving, you give up your right of redress or compensation for the harm done to you. Why it is like that, and what is the gift aspect? It is inherent in Biblical literature that we should forgive people who trespass against us. As you forgive that person, that forgiveness becomes a heavenly giving. Does the receiver of that gift deserve it? The answer is no; the receiver does not deserve it, and the receiver may not even want that gift even as he or she receives it. Forgiveness is a priceless gift that no amount of money can buy. In case you are still confused, forgiveness is paying with kindness for the evil done to you. To be able

BEING IN LOVE, STAYING IN LOVE, AND GROWING IN LOVE

to forgive anybody, the relationship between you and God must come first. As you remember your own trespasses that God forgave you, likewise you can and should be able to forgive others, including your spouse. When you forgive, let go, remembering that Christ forgave you, and He never came back to rescind that forgiveness.

Love must be learned, and learned again and again; there is no end to it.
—Katherine Ann Porter

CHAPTER THREE

Building And Maintaining Marriages

A successful marriage is one in which requires falling in love many times, always with the same person.

—McLaughlin

MARRIAGE IS THE coming together of a man and woman, pledging their love and unity to each other in perpetuity, regardless of the circumstance. As for the objectives of marriage, they include procreation, intimacy, unity, companionship, commitment, and comfort. Let us review each objective and its applicability to marriage.

Procreation

This objective enables the couple to have children and enjoy the process of raising a family. The joy and rewards of having and caring for a family are immense and unparalleled. The genealogical family tree continues, and the fulfillment of God's directive about "increasing and multiplying" is achieved as the couple does their share of helping in reasonable and meaningful population of the earth.

LOVE AND MARRIAGE PERSPECTIVES

Intimacy and passion

This is one of the rewards and unique gifts of marriage. The couple shares with each other, including their thoughts and feelings and sexual intimacy, at the deepest levels. Intimacy and passion are key ingredients of marriage. Some couples misinterpret intimacy and passion as sex, sex, and more sex. I am not advocating that sex is not part of a marriage, for it is. What I am stating, or am about to state below, is that there is a time and a place for everything. That a certain sequential order has to be followed for intimacy and passion to have meaning in a marriage. Intimacy has to lead to passion, for seeking passion first, without intimacy, would be like putting the cart before the horse.

Intimacy has to do with how you understand your partner. Ask yourself the following: How well do I know this individual? Are we equally yoked? Are we similar or dissimilar? Assuming there is dissimilarity, what do I want from this person? What type of personality does this person have? What makes this person tick? What are his or her strengths and weaknesses? How does he or she handle anger or manage conflict? What are my fears about this individual? Am I able to cope with this person in certain situations? Do I really love this person, or am I just infatuated or just going with emotions? Will I be passionate with this person? Will I have sexual satisfaction with this person?

As you begin to review the above questions and process your findings or answers, you start to have the idea of the deep meaning of intimacy. Intimacy is that unique closeness or bonding with your partner, and the foundation of intimacy is laid during the courtship stage. It is the exploration and sharing of your innermost thoughts and deepest feelings with your partner. With this sharing and exploration, we tend to understand our partners and even ourselves better. The mystery of marriage starts unfolding, and you and your partner have reached a genuine intimacy. When you reach the stage of genuine intimacy in a marriage, other parts of the puzzle will start falling into place and the relationship will run like a well-oiled machine. At this point in the relationship, sex is meaningful and enjoyable. It becomes further intertwined with the marriage and is an intricate part of the marriage relationship.

Passion is the gift of marriage. Some people get married but never experience true passion. True passion in marriage means the couple has reached the point where they can truly experience and enjoy sex fully in the context of the marital relationship.

Unity

In marriage, two people and two bodies are united together, and they become one flesh. The couple is now one soul, or soul mates, by virtue of being one flesh. The two think as one, living together in unity. They eat together, raise their children together, and go though their triumphs as well as their trials and tribulations together.

LOVE AND MARRIAGE PERSPECTIVES

Companionship

After creating man, God noted what a terrible life man would have without a companion. So in Genesis 2:18, he stated:

> *It is not good that man should be alone; I will make him a helper comparable to him.*

The creation of a woman from the ribs of a man accomplished the objective of God finding a companion comparable to him, hence his woman, his wife, tailor-made for him from his own ribs. What an amazing and wonderful thing from God. The objective of companionship was further illustrated in Ecclesiastes 4:9–10:

> *Two are better than one, because they have a good reward for their labor. For if they fall, one will lift up his companion.*

Commitment

Commitment is the unique understanding that all of your body and soul are absolutely and wholeheartedly reserved for and devoted to your spouse. In marriage, visualize the type of marriage that you want. Have aspirations together, no secret agendas. Do not withhold from your spouse, for if you do, you are not fully giving yourself to your spouse. By not giving yourself fully, you are cheating or robbing your marriage of the commitment to which it is entitled. Your marriage will not be fulfilling. Always

BUILDING AND MAINTAINING MARRIAGES

be inclusive. See your spouse as your other half; in that situation, you are complete. Remember that you are sharing, or are supposed to be sharing, your life with your spouse. If not, if you are withholding and keeping certain things to yourself, you are only robbing yourself and your spouse of love. To be deeply in love, you have to give yourself to your spouse fully. To achieve this sharing of life, there must be commitment. When both partners are committed, their bonding becomes unique; however, they should work toward achieving deep commitment.

Commitment is that bonding you get when you and your spouse are open to each other and discuss issues without withholding. Your spouse is your friend. Deep commitment is when you take it further, when you and your spouse are not only friends but the best of friends, super bonded and sharing your innermost feelings. Your spouse even understands you by looking into your eyes, understanding your nonverbal communication.

Comfort

Comfort is the peace of mind, enjoyment, enrichment, relaxation, and fulfillment one gets by following every dictate, tenet, and requirement of his or her marriage vows. Living by your vows has rights and privileges, for there is nothing that your spouse will not give you if you ask for it. Both of you are happy and comfortable with each other by living with the rules of marriage. Regarding comfort, Ecclesiastes 4:11 says the following:

Again, if two lie down together, they will keep warm; but how can one be warm alone?

Living one day at a time or planning?

Some people advocate that you should live one day at a time in marriage. I do not agree with living one day at a time in a marriage. Why? In marriage, it is all about planning. I will give you two slogans: (1) If you do not have a plan in marriage, then you plan to fail; (2) A fool with a plan in a marriage is smarter than a genius who is in a marriage with no plan.

Planning is everything in marriage. You and your spouse work out all your goals and objectives in a marriage. When two people plan something together and agree on it, there is a strong probability of success since both are parties to that plan. Your spouse does not doubt where you are coming from; there is clarity in what both of you planned together. There is the least likelihood of conflict because you are implementing the plan that both of you agreed on. Even when conflict occurs, it can be easily resolved if the cause of the conflict is a result of the objective or action in your plans since no plan or nothing is perfect. If there is conflict even with plans, can you then imagine when you and your spouse operate with no plans? Successful marriages do not just happen; they require decisions, planning, skills, and great willingness to make the marriage work.

Again, commitment ensures strength in marriage. It is the foundation of a good and healthy love or marriage relationship. The meaning of your marriage vows to you, or how seriously you take those vows, and the type of bonding with your partner, determine the likely success or failure of your marriage.

Strive for love

Make sure you love the individual whom you are marrying. Some may have childhood dreams of marrying only a physician or attorney and may miss out on some good prospects. Even if you should meet and marry that physician, that person's occupation by itself does not necessarily guarantee a good marriage. Let love be your guiding principle as to whom you marry.

Someone who agrees with you or is similar to you

Each individual has his or her own sophistication and complexities. Can you imagine when those two individuals want to come together to become one? That is a web of complexities. Make sure the individual likes what you like, and so forth. Conflicts are more easily resolved when people are alike.

How about trust?

When you trust somebody, you can open up yourself in discussing issues with that person. Can you then imagine if you are in love and also trust your lover? The degree of openness is endless, for with trust, you can open yourself to your lover or spouse fully, freely, entirely, and absolutely. What a beautiful thing when a couple has that type of understanding and can share their innermost thoughts and feelings.

Why is trust important in a relationship?

It lets people be themselves and creates an avenue where a couple can discuss or share feelings with no reservations. It solidifies a marriage when two people trust each other and are working toward the same objective. Trust gives feelings of oneness and keeps you and your spouse on the same page. You feel a sense of accomplishment in knowing that you are following your marriage plans that you and your spouse set up to accomplish. Trust further provides a forum where you believe in your partner, knowing that not only can you trust your spouse, but depend on him or her as well. It is the glue that binds a relationship. When trust is present in a marital relationship, truth manifests, and lies becomes a thing of the past. We were admonished in Ephesians 4:25 as follows:

> *Putting away lying, let each one of you speak the truth with his neighbor, for we are members of one another.*

When truth is absent from a relationship, whether it is a marriage or a dating relationship, it shows that the core or the foundation of that relationship has what I call a structural defect. A relationship cannot be meaningful with lies, conniving, deceitfulness, cheating, dishonesty, and doing things behind your partner's back. Those factors hinder a relationship. A relationship that is grounded in deceitfulness is like a hurricane waiting to make landfall. The consequence of that landfall will be disastrous. It is like a ship on a voyage with no rudder and sinking. A marriage that is deceitful with hidden agendas will also sink. When trust is broken, the relationship is no longer fulfilling.

The main key in restoring trust is to be honest with your partner by discussing issues openly. Do not rationalize or be defensive. It may take some sessions of psychotherapy, depending on the precipitating factors. The aggrieved partner should try to forgive the spouse who violated the trust, if he or she asks for forgiveness. The Lord's Prayer states, "Forgive us our trespasses as we forgive those who trespassed against us." You have less stress in the marriage or the relationship if there is trust. You do not have to waste your time being suspicious or worrying about what your partner is doing. You relax and have peace of mind and devote your energy to other positive activities.

Chemistry

When two people in love experience chemistry, the relationship is on the right track. Chemistry is the vital catalyst that makes the fundamentals of a relationship operate with relative ease. With chemistry, conflicts are less likely to occur, and when they do, they can be resolved in a flash. Couples get along better and see themselves together. Bonding is easier, and other technicalities of a relationship fall into place with chemistry.

Some chemistry can be natural, in that you meet someone, and as you communicate, you find out that both of you are similar. That type of situation is ideal, and a relationship like that has a strong propensity to succeed. But even if a couple doesn't have chemistry initially, two people in a relationship can develop and enhance it. Chemistry can be built or injected in a relationship with time, understanding, mutual respect, love, and passion, especially when two people in a relationship honestly want chemistry and are willing to work for it. However, it will be more difficult to build chemistry in a fragile or vulnerable relationship. Take into consideration that no relationship is perfect, and the degree of chemistry in a relationship depends on the individuals in that relationship.

Chemistry and a sense of perception are closely linked. Chemistry shows the extent to which individuals in a relationship are connected or understand each other. For example, one partner might be shopping and see an outfit that he or she knows the other partner will like. That spouse buys it, and on getting home, the other spouse likes it so much, as if the partner that bought it read the other's mind. Chemistry can be exhibited through nonverbal communication, where one partner looks at the other and knows what he or she wants. Chemistry can also be feelings, the way each partner feels toward the other.

BUILDING AND MAINTAINING MARRIAGES

Marriage requires work

Working on marriage starts immediately after the honeymoon. Most marriages get into trouble when one or both spouses feel content just being married, feeling that nothing is required to maintain the marriage. An acquaintance of mine was so happy when he was married. He shared how it was difficult initially—the amount of work he did to get his then fiancée, now his wife, to go out with him. He further mentioned the amount of energy he put into planning the wedding. My acquaintance concluded that he was happy that all his work was now over—that his job was finished. He felt that all he had to do from then on was go home and eat, make love to his wife, and go to sleep. I curiously asked him how he was going to maintain his marriage to ensure that the tempo of the marriage did not regress. He asked what I meant by maintenance. Let us review the issue of maintenance in a marriage.

Marriage maintenance

I advised my acquaintance that marriage maintenance is similar to the way he maintains his car to ensure that it runs the way that it is supposed to run. Let us assume that his name is Carl. I said, "Carl, think about that new car you bought prior to your wedding. If you look at the owner's manual, you'll see that it states what needs to be done at certain miles. Specifically, the oil has to be changed at certain times. There are tune-ups, change of belts, tire rotation, and things like that. It's the same with marriage. If marriage is not maintained, it will fall apart in the same way

LOVE AND MARRIAGE PERSPECTIVES

your car will if not maintained." Carl stated that what I was saying appeared to make sense, and that he had not seen it that way previously. Marriages need maintenance and work. Anderson and Anderson (2003, 177) stated: "Making a marriage work is like a farm. You start working it all over again each morning."

Maintaining a marriage enhances passion, understanding, communication, and sharing. It also enhances continuity and love. Regarding love, Anderson and Anderson (2003, 7) further noted: "But the two love each other so much that they allow nothing to stand in the way. They sacrifice all to satisfy each other's needs. They overcome every obstacle to be together. They resolve every conflict and forgive every wrong."

Simply stated, marriage maintenance ensures bonding and lets you know your spouse more and better. Knowing him or her better ensures a smoother, more meaningful marriage. According to a respondent to their survey, Stains and Bechtel (2000, 423) noted the following regarding marriage maintenance: "We have been married for twenty-four years. We have a strong marriage. My spouse is my best friend, and I love him. We work at our marriage every day and do not take each other for granted. We feel that we are on our second honeymoon since the kids have grown up. Life is great."

All these tend to buttress the importance of maintaining your marriage on a daily basis. Marriage is a full-time job, not a part-time one.

Expression of Love

Different couples express love differently. The way that expression of love is received is also different. The key point here is that in marriage, love has to be expressed to get the full meaning and effect of marriage. A marriage in which love is not being expressed is like bland food with no flavor or seasoning. A husband or a wife wants to know how he or she is performing in a marriage. I do not mean sexual performance—I am referring to the details of everyday things that happen in a marriage. Can you imagine taking a test in your school days and never knowing what you scored? Wouldn't that elevate your anxiety level?

Conditions for expressing love

We should always make the conditions right for our spouses to express love. Those conditions include appreciation or praising, unconditional love, and fight-or-flight syndrome. Let us review each one of these conditions and how it impacts marriage.

Appreciation or praising

The premise for this is from the theory of operant conditioning, in which people repeat a certain behavior when rewarded or praised. In marriage, when you praise your spouse, he or she will love you more, share more, and open up his or her heart more. It's the same with appreciation. When a spouse feels appreciated, that spouse doubles his or her effort toward the success of the marriage. An example is appropriate here. At tennis practice, Marx was discussing how happy his marriage is, and how he gets everything he wants from his wife, Rosa. Gustav, who was at the same practice, wanted to know how he accomplished that, saying that he did not have such luck in his marriage. Marx said he showed his appreciation by telling her what a wonderful bride she is. Marx felt lucky to have married her—that Rosa was the best thing that ever happened to him. And he always let her know that. Mark said that the praising and appreciation made his marriage better. Rosa gave him sex without reservation and always wanted to know what would make Marx happy so she could do that. Rosa was able to express her love liberally.

Concerning appreciation and praising, a respondent to Stains and Bechtel (2000, 146) put it more succinctly: "My husband always makes me feel special. The little things are a real turn-on. I like being touched and told I am loved. Being thankful for things I do and say helped a lot, lets me know how much he cares."

Fight-or-flight syndrome

In the animal kingdom, when animals are faced with conflict, they either fight or flee. In marriage, we can set up a condition wherein our spouses sense security in the marriage. When a spouse has a feeling of security, he or she can express love freely. If a spouse thinks that the environment of the marriage is conductive for expression of love, that spouse will express love unreservedly. If a spouse senses a situation or an environment that lacks security, he or she will be inhibited from expressing love.

Let us look at the case of Rio and Ruby, who have been married for over a year. Rio is frustrated because he believes that Ruby does not love him the way he feels that she should. Rio is of the opinion that Ruby was withholding and probably had an affair with an ex-boyfriend named Renaldo, who was in town a few months earlier. Rio was establishing a correlation between Ruby's withholding and Renaldo's visit. Rio employed the help of Ruby's best friend, Lupe, to find out why Ruby had been withholding. Ruby had confided in Lupe that she talked to Renaldo when he was in town. She declined Renaldo's invitation for lunch because she did not want to rekindle anything with him. Ruby stated to Lupe that she wanted to tell Rio what transpired, but Rio always threatened her with divorce over little things, such as when he perceived that a meal was not cooked right. She said that she loves Rio, but that love is now out of fear.

In this situation, Rio created a hostile love environment, wherein Ruby perceived no security in her marriage. She did not have an affair but was withholding out of fear, in an attempt to save her marriage. Ruby did not want to fight Rio; she instead chose to flee from the situation. We should always provide our spouses with an atmosphere of security to enable them to articulate their feelings without any fear of reprisal.

LOVE AND MARRIAGE PERSPECTIVES

Unconditional love

I will start this section on unconditional love with a story from *The Maury Povich Show*. For the purpose of this book, a couple hereinafter known as Nelson and Hilda came to the show. Hilda wanted Nelson to take a lie detector test because she suspected that he was cheating on her. When Nelson was introduced, there was a long pause, and during the absolute silence, jaws were dropping. The reason was that Nelson was completely disfigured facially because of third-degree burns he sustained when his apartment caught on fire. Maury asked Nelson if he was cheating on Hilda. Nelson's response was not only was he not cheating on Hilda, but even if he wanted to cheat, nobody would want him. When Maury asked why, he said, "Look at my disfigured face." Nelson had gone through twenty-two surgeries and skin grafts. His face remained grossly disfigured despite those surgeries. Even with that disfiguration, when Hilda was asked if she loved Nelson, her response was that Nelson was handsome, and that she loved him unconditionally. She rose from her seat and sat with Nelson, kissing him passionately and yelling, "This is my man." The audience cheered her on. The lie detector test showed that he was not cheating. Nelson knelt on one knee and proposed to Hilda. She accepted. That is what I call unconditional love.

Writing about unconditional love, Lepine (1999, 153) stated: "The life of Hosea is a living illustration of the unconditional love of God, who chose to love us, not because we have earned or deserved his love, but because it pleases him to love us." With unconditional love, your spouse knows that he or she is loved regardless of the circumstances. That environment of unconditional love opens up your spouse to love you back the same way, also without any reservations. The reason for that love and openness is that the marriage provided a conductive environment for that type of expression of love.

Throughout our discussion of expression of love, a key word that keeps coming up is sharing. Let us review the significance of sharing in love expression.

Sharing

Sharing is a method of expressing love. It is also a method of communication. When you do not share, your marriage is superficial. The danger in a superficial marriage is that there is no in-depth commitment. You are depriving your spouse of intimate communication when you do not share, or when you share only partially. It is a serious flaw in a marriage when either or both spouses are not sharing.

Sharing in marriage should be real, open, and complete. It should also be free, without duress or any kind of intimidation. Any deviation from that defeats the purpose of marriage. When a spouse is withholding in marriage, there is a high probability that the withholding spouse is hiding something. If he or she is not hiding something that is detrimental to the marriage, why is that spouse not articulating? Such a marriage is unhealthy. In a healthy marriage, both spouses normally express what is on their minds.

Sharing also builds trust. Would you like to be in a marriage where your spouse does not trust you? The quickest way to earn that trust in your marriage is by sharing at the deepest levels so you are revealing your sincere feelings, emotions, and desires. Sharing shows absolute and full confidence in your marriage and your spouse. Your marriage is super healthy at that level, and your needs are also met at the highest level. That is how important sharing is in marriage.

Regarding trust, sharing, and self-disclosure, Kelly et al. (2003, 444), noted: "By engaging in strong levels of self-disclosure, one communicates trust in the partner, who in turn tends to reciprocate such disclosures. Hence, self-disclosure can be largely understood in terms of enhancing interdependence, a pattern of interaction that is often initiated by one partner and reciprocated by the other."

Challenges in a marriage

Marriage can be a challenge. Several factors contribute to the challenges in marriage. The maturity level of the couples involved in the marriage goes a long way in ameliorating or alleviating these challenges. Some of these challenges include faithfulness in the marriage, the presence or absence of life-changing events, and the types of friends you have in the marriage. Let us review the issues and explore how they impact marriage.

Faithfulness versus unfaithfulness

This is also known as fidelity versus infidelity. Most people who get married do so with the intention of remaining faithful. This is because initially a relationship is full of passion and romance. In the course of a marriage, some people may start feeling differently about their marriage, especially if they entered into the marriage with an ulterior motive other than love. When a spouse feels that the marriage is no longer meeting his or her needs, the mind or heart and the eyes start to wander. At this point, things in the marriage start falling apart, and the core of the marriage weakens. This is the stage where infidelity creeps into the marriage, for the foundation of that infidelity was laid first with the mind. Once the notion is hatched in the mind, the individual starts acting out his or her feelings, and the person's extramarital relationship will have damaging consequences for the marriage relationship.

Life-changing events

A couple can be so much in love that in the eyes of their neighbors, all seems to be going well in the marriage. But let's assume that one spouse has a stroke and has to be confined to a wheelchair. Assuming that their bonding is not fully grounded and deep, and the healthy spouse decides to leave the marriage, can you imagine the fate of the marriage, especially if there are children involved? Can you further imagine the types of challenges the sick spouse has to face—as well as what the whole scenario has done to this union?

Friends with the opposite sex

I had a discussion with a friend of mine on the appropriateness of a married person having a friend of the opposite sex outside of the marriage. According to my friend, there was no sexual relationship involved. His rationale in this regard was that he needed someone to talk to for stress management. Consider this illustration: Let us imagine that Steve is married to Shay. Steve has a female friend, Jane, whom he talks to off and on. Shay was unaware of Steve's friendship with Jane until Steve's cell phone rang one evening at dinnertime. Steve looked at the number but did not want to take the call. Shay wanted to know why Steve was not answering his phone. Steve stated that it was probably a telemarketer. Shay asked how Steve knew that the call was from a telemarketer. Steve's response was that they mostly call in the evenings, when people are home from their jobs. After dinner, when Shay came to the bedroom to get something, she overheard Steve in the bathroom talking to a female, who incidentally happened to be Jane, on his cell phone. Shay confronted Steve after his call. Steve denied that he was talking to a female, until Shay told Steve some of the words he'd used during the call. As their discussion progressed, Steve admitted that he was talking to Jane. According to Steve, Jane was just a friend; they worked in the same building but not in the same office or for the same company. They talked about general issues, and there was no sex involved. Steve told Shay that he'd never told her about Jane because he did not want to upset her. In short, they were friends with no "benefits," meaning sexual relations.

Appropriateness of outside friendships

I do not see anything wrong with married people having a friend of the opposite sex so long as the other spouse is aware of it, the terms of the friendship are clearly established, and the other spouse approves of such a friendship. What is not right is when one spouse has a friend outside the marriage and hides it from the other spouse. There is also some danger in even the friendship approved by the other spouse, if some derogatory information were excluded at the time of that approval. That spouse approved the friendship based on the information given by his or her spouse. What if the other spouse misrepresented the true objective of his or her friendship with the opposite sex? Friendship with the opposite sex outside the marriage should be pursued with caution and is more likely to hurt a marriage than help it. Let us process the case of Steve and Shay. It would also be a good idea to discuss how issues like that affect a marriage as a whole.

In the case of Steve, whenever a spouse starts hiding issues or withholding from the other spouse, there is something wrong with that picture. If not properly addressed, that withholding is perhaps the beginning of the end of that marriage. Steve had no plans to tell Shay until he was caught talking on his cell phone. When spouses start discussing issues and one spouse lies about the situation, it does not augur well for the marriage. This reminds me of a person who was having extramarital affairs and decided to come partially clean to his wife, admitting to a one-time sexual indiscretion. It was later learned that he was involved with this woman for a number of years, and the so-called one-night stand was not true. If your spouse has a friend of the opposite sex whom he or she is talking to behind your back, that is a red flag in your marriage.

Some red flags

There are some issues or points—or, more appropriately, some red flags—to consider. In marriage, your spouse should be the one you can't wait to get home to and discuss how your day went, including what happened at work. Your spouse is the person with whom you share everything going on in your life. Your spouse is also the person you should be spending time with, and I'm not referring just to sexual time spent together.

When one spouse spends time with or talks with a member of the opposite sex and states that there is no sex involved, it is probably not true. This is a red flag in the marriage. Even if Steve and Jane are not having sex, Shay is being robbed of the emotional bonding that her marriage should bestow on her. When one spouse starts talking to a friend of the opposite sex, he or she is depriving the other spouse of emotional bonding. Take into account that marriage is about sharing emotions and feelings. For Steve to leave Shay and share some of his emotions with Jane does not augur well for his marriage.

When one spouse diverts any emotion from the other spouse and shares that emotion or feeling with a friend of the opposite sex outside the marriage, it is an emotional wreck for the other spouse. As you share your emotions, you bond with that friend. The more that spouse continues to share, the more the bonding with the outside friend. There is a correlation between emotional sharing and emotional bonding. That outside bonding due to outside sharing is the bonding being taken away from the marriage. There is an attraction between two friends of the opposite sex in order for them to be friends and share in the first place. Take into account that before you married your spouse, it started as friendship and then progressed to romance. So what is there to prevent your outside friendship from doing the same? The attraction is already there for both of you if you are friends and even share issues. Any amount of time taken out of the marriage to share with your outside friend of the opposite sex hurts your marriage, and it is up to you to make the decision as to the extent to which you want to hurt your marriage by that outside intrusion.

It is worth it having outside friends in marriage?

Whether it is worth having outside friends of the opposite sex in

LOVE AND MARRIAGE PERSPECTIVES

marriage depends on the spouse who wants that outside friendship. My questions to that spouse: What is your marriage worth to you? Do you value your outside friend more than your husband or wife? What can that outside friendship do for you that your wife or husband cannot do for you? I keep using the words "outside friendship" because your spouse is already your friend, so what do you need another friend of the opposite sex for? If your marriage is worth nothing to you and you have a need for outside friendship after reviewing the questions above, you probably married the wrong person. If you did not marry the wrong person, then you married for the wrong reasons.

A girlfriend from my high school years discussed with me that she was trying to divorce her husband, and she gave the following scenario. Let us assume that her name is Mary and the husband is Joe. Mary advised that she was about to divorce Joe because he had a bad understanding regarding her friend Paul. My heart stopped for a second when she named a male as her friend, because friends of the opposite sex are sometimes a disaster in marriage. According to Mary, Joe wanted her to stop her friendship with Paul. Mary was furious because her relationship with Paul was platonic—no sex was involved. Since Paul had been married longer than she had, talking to him gave her understanding regarding marital issues. Paul, according to her, gave her balanced issues and let her compare things in marriage, thereby giving her an understanding of how to relate with Joe. Let us process what is wrong with this scenario.

BUILDING AND MAINTAINING MARRIAGES

In marriage, comparing notes with what is happening in your friends' marriages and yours can be misleading and wrong. We have already discussed that your spouse should be your friend. We also explored how outside friendship can lead to other things. The danger when you start comparing marriages is that each marriage is different, and individuals in marriage are also different. No two marriages are alike, and seeking what is in another person's marriage causes undue stress because there can be no true comparison. It may make a little more sense if a married female is comparing with another married female—but not with a friend of the opposite sex. Your outside friend may want more than friendship, which may probably result in sexual feelings. The danger is that whenever sex is introduced in any friendship, it clouds the ability for that friend to be unbiased in whatever input you are getting. Your marriage suffers even when sex is not involved. Daly (2009, 117) noted the following: "Simply avoiding sex may not be enough to protect your primary relationship."

I do not think that it is worth doing anything that will affect your marriage. Mary stopped her association with Paul. Her marriage with Joe recovered, and they moved on with their lives.

It is devastating for any spouse when his or her partner has those types of outside emotional attachments. Daly (2009), quoting Manex in a Florida State University (2008) study, observed that "94% of women said that if their partner became involved with someone else, they'd be more upset if he bonded emotionally with that woman than if he bonded physically."

LOVE AND MARRIAGE PERSPECTIVES

When it comes to emotional attachment by either spouse, it is a marriage breaker. Maner (2009, 117) noted: "From an evolutionary standpoint, the possibility of a man investing his affection, energy, and resources in someone else is a big reproductive threat for a woman, even bigger than the possibility of his engaging in casual sex."

Some marital strategies to consider

(1) Resolve conflicts quickly and meaningfully. Always use the power of negotiation. Remember that your spouse is your equal partner. Do not talk down to or at him or her. Let meaningful compromise be your guide.

(2) Do not express your anger impulsively. Think before you speak or act or you may end up regretting the outcome of your actions. Proverbs 14:29 says, "He who is slow to wrath has great understanding, but he who is impulsive exalts folly." Furthermore, Proverbs 15:18 says, "A wrathful man stirs up strife, but he who is slow to anger allays contention."

(3) Marriage is not always peaches and cream. As with anything in life, there are bound to be ups and downs. There are bound to be disappointments. The way you handle those disappointments sometimes determines the direction and flow of your marriage. It can make or break it.

(4) Avoid things, people, or places that will hurt your spouse's

BUILDING AND MAINTAINING MARRIAGES

feelings. Remember that what is good for the goose is also good for the gander. If it does not feel right, do not do it. You might regret it. You might even want to take it back, which is impossible, for what is done cannot be undone, and what is bad is bad, no matter who does it.

(5) There may be a time when your spouse rejects you, even your affections. Explore the reasons or the circumstances for the rejection or refusal. Assuming it is a result of your own actions, apologize not superficially but profusely. It is said in Proverbs 15:1, "A soft answer turns away wrath, but a harsh word stirs up anger."

(6) Always talk to your spouse respectfully, regardless of the situation or circumstance. Remember that respect is reciprocal—give and receive.

(7) At all times, watch what you say to your spouse. Remember that he or she is your better half, and both of you are one. The book of Proverbs 13:3 stated, "He who guards his mouth preserves his life, but he who opens wide his lips shall have destruction."

(8) If you are the husband, I know that you would like to claim your place as the head of the family, but in order to do so; you need to model appropriate behavior and take responsibility for things that went wrong in your marriage.

(9) Never, I repeat *never*, put your hands on your wife for any reason. Regardless of the circumstance, there are several ways

LOVE AND MARRIAGE PERSPECTIVES

to resolve conflict in marriage, and violence is not one of them. Verbal abuse should also be avoided at all costs. Conflicts should be resolved through verbal means and compromise.

(10) Always be truthful with each other. When you lie to your spouse, you are lying to yourself. You are also tearing down your marriage, which both of you have likely invested a lot of time and effort to develop. Besides, if you tell a lie, you have to tell another lie to cover up the first lie you told. Before you know it, your marriage is degraded because of lies, and it will probably crumble or succumb because of those lies. Your marriage is no longer straightforward. Ecclesiastes 1:15 says, "What is crooked cannot be made straight, and what is lacking cannot be numbered." Ecclesiastes 1:15.

(11) Nothing wrecks a marriage like sexual indiscretion, being unfaithful to your spouse. Cheating robs the heart and soul of the spouse that was cheated on. Marital infidelity, as far as being cheated on, is one area in which most people lose rational thinking. It can cost you your marriage, your home, and almost everything that you worked for within the marriage. It is not worth it, so do not do it.

(12) Your marriage largely depends on your attitude. There is a saying that attitude is everything. Why? The answer is that attitude influences our actions. Actions influence our emotions. Emotions influence our thinking processes, which in turn influence our behaviors. One may ask where perception is in all of

BUILDING AND MAINTAINING MARRIAGES

this. Answer: It goes back to attitude. Remember that attitude is everything—the catalyst that sets the whole process into motion.

(13) When you forgive your spouse, try to let go completely. Do not keep bringing up issues that you already forgave. Otherwise, you will be stuck and never move on. Remember, as you forgive others, so shall you be forgiven.

(14) Always compliment each other. The wife, for example, may want to thank the husband for taking out the trash after dinner. The husband may compliment his wife by saying, "Honey, you look so great today." You may be surprised what complimenting each other can do for your marriage.

(15) Marriage is all about learning. That is why marriage is a journey, a process, a mystery, and a puzzle. The more you lean about this process, the smoother the road on this journey becomes. The more involved you are in your marriage, the more understanding you have with your spouse. It is a good idea to attend marriage seminars or read books or articles on marriage from reputable magazines.

(16) Marriage is not a fantasy world. It involves hard work, commitment, and courage. Marriage has good rewards and benefits, but these do not just come to you. Both of you have to work for them.

LOVE AND MARRIAGE PERSPECTIVES

(17) You will be amazed what a dozen roses will do for your marriage. Get the flowers delivered to your spouse's place of work. The roses will speak for themselves, and her colleagues will tell the rest of the story.

(18) Do not underestimate the power of giving gifts, especially on birthdays, anniversaries, Valentine's Day, and other special holidays. I vividly remember a friend of mine telling me that his wife put him out of the bedroom for forgetting her birthday. Note that it is not what is given, but the spirit in which it is given.

(19) Make God a priority in your marriage. Putting God first makes it easier to work on issues couples may confront in the marriage. Consider being prayerful with your spouse. The family that prays together stays together. That habit of praying will also be passed on to your children, for they will learn that Jesus taught us what follows in the Gospel according to John: "If I then, your Lord and teacher, have washed your feet, you also ought to wash one another's feet. For I have given you an example, that you should do as I have done to you. If you know these things, blessed are you if you do them." John 13:14–15, 17.

(20) Do not spend impulsively. Save for that rainy day, for it will surely come. Practice budgeting and other fiscal measures. Manage your finances and investment portfolios wisely. Living within your means is a good strategy.

(21) As much as possible, help your wife with chores around the

house. I am not talking about fixing a leaking faucet or washing the car. If you can wash the car, you can wash the dishes or at least put them in the dishwasher. Sometimes it is the little things that matter.

(22) Avoid judgmental listening by withholding judgment when your spouse is talking. It is a good practice to allow him or her to finish, giving you clarity about your spouse's position on the issues. Rushing to judgment without a complete grasp of the facts solves nothing and only shows your impulsivity on issues. Not only does this practice stop the flow of communication by interrupting your spouse, but you pronounce judgment based on your own incomplete view of the situation.

(23) Practice working out issues with your spouse instead of walking out on issues from your spouse. The problem does not go away because you walk out. It does nothing but increase or aggravates the situation.

(24) Try to be part of the solution rather than part of the problem. Avoid situations that will bring hostility, discord, pain, and misunderstanding to your marriage. It is better to be proactive than reactive. "The beginning of strife is like releasing water; therefore stop contention before a quarrel starts." (Proverbs 17:14)

(25) Accept constructive criticism from each other. You may have the best intentions in your heart on certain actions, decisions, or

LOVE AND MARRIAGE PERSPECTIVES

stands you may take in your marriage. It is, however, good to know how your spouse perceives you and your stand on issues.

(26) Work as a team. Remember, you are now one flesh. Recognize each other's achievements and accomplishments. It does not matter who has achieved the most. Her achievements are yours, and his achievements are yours. Support each other, for you are not in competition. It does not matter who earns more money or who has the better job. As the saying goes, it's all in the family.

(27) Jealousy can ruin a marriage. There is healthy jealousy, and there is unhealthy jealousy. Do not let your unhealthy jealousy influence you to start fishing for issues or situations that do not even exist. Be careful not to tread on thin ice in this area.

(28) Always be hopeful that things will get better in your marriage. If your marriage is bad, strive for it to be good. If your marriage is good, strive for it to be better. If your marriage is better, congratulations—now work toward making it the best marriage. There is no hopeless marriage, in that if you can make the decision to marry your spouse, you saw some good at the beginning, and that can still be salvaged. An attitude of hopelessness and despair does not go well in marriage.

(29) Avoid doing things behind each other's backs. Do not withhold things, for doing so robs each other of sharing the deepest thoughts, emotions, and feelings. This is taking away the key ingredient that binds marriages, which is sharing.

(30) Never leave issues unresolved for too long. The danger is that hurt feelings affect emotions, and when emotions are affected for a period of time, couples start drifting apart, and with that, feelings and affections start changing.

(31) In spite of your busy schedule, it important to adjust your schedule to make time for meaningful, quality time with your spouse. This is the time designated for you and your spouse to spend together. Assuming you have children, consider making arrangements for babysitting sometimes. During this time, rediscover your sex life. There is no rushing. Yes, spice it up, for it enhances marriage.

(32) You will be amazed at the degree of closeness you and your spouse can have when you go through life-changing events together. Some people call this being emotionally available for each other in critical situations. A life-changing event is just that—it changes your life. It could be loss of a job, sickness such as cancer, a downward spiral in income, a serious accident, or the loss of a loved one. If both of you got stuck together by being there for each other, that marriage has survived a catastrophic event and the tendency for that marriage to last longer is high because of the survival of that event.

(33) Communicate, communicate, and communicate your feelings to each other. If you notice, I used the word communicate three consecutive times to stress the importance of communication in a marriage. It is better to talk it out than act out.

LOVE AND MARRIAGE PERSPECTIVES

(34) Be tolerant and patient with each other. During my undergraduate years in college, I had a key chain that read PATIENCE IS A VIRTUE. I bought that keychain at a fancy high-rise mall. During my graduate years, I was at a dollar store and saw a similar key chain with this inscription: OH, LORD, GRANT ME PATIENCE, BUT HURRY. I instantly related to it. The reason behind that story is to illustrate the importance of patience in our dealings with others, especially in marriage. Knowing the importance of patience, why did I all of a sudden want patience in a hurry? Patience is not hurried, but something to wait for. As it says in the Bible, "Now may the God of patience and comfort grant you to be like-minded toward one another, according to Christ Jesus." (Romans 15:5)

(35) Trust is a key element in marriage. When trust is stronger, the marital relationship is stronger. Avoid things that will erode trust in your marriage. Once trust is broken, it is always difficult to get that trust back. With no trust in your marriage, it appears that you may be beginning to look at the possible end of your marriage.

(36) Do not hold grudges against each other. This may lead to aggression. Process hostile feelings together to help in knowing what went wrong, how it went wrong and the best way to correct it. Do not act impulsively; always think of the likely consequences of your actions. Learn how to handle frustrating situations without overreacting.

(37) A quick or hot temper is a ticking time bomb in marriage,

BUILDING AND MAINTAINING MARRIAGES

for it is only a question of time before it explodes. Why? In marriage, you deal with people's feelings and emotions -- those and quick temper do not go together. So finding ways and means of controlling your temper is a good idea. Proverbs 14:17 states, "A quick-tempered man acts foolishly."

(38) Express affection toward each other. If you love your spouse, show it. If you love your spouse, say it. If you love your spouse, act as if you do. Actions speak louder than words.

(39) While there are certain issues that fall within the purview of a licensed professional counselor, it is not a bad idea to seek each other's counsel in daily events in your life, both at home and in your jobs. Seeking each other's counsel not only binds both of you together, but it keeps you in tune and in touch with the daily occurrences in your lives. The Bible stated in Proverbs 12:15, "But he who heeds counsel is wise."

(40) Finally, each marriage is unique, and each spouse is unique, with his or her own personality and respective God-given talents, skills, and abilities. What works for one marriage may not work for another. Identify what works for you and your spouse and use that as a frame of reference. Improve on it and make your marriage a passion of happiness.

I will close this section on strategies to consider in marriage situations with a quote from the Epistle of Paul the Apostle to the Philippians:

LOVE AND MARRIAGE PERSPECTIVES

Finally, brethren, whatever things are true, whatever things are noble, whatever things are just, whatever things are pure, whatever things are lovely, whatever things are of good report, if there is any virtue and if there is anything praiseworthy—meditate on these things. The things which you learned and received and heard and saw in me, these do, and the God of peace will be with you. (Philippians 4:8–9)

Marriage is like the army. Everybody complains, but you'd be surprised at how many re-enlist.

—Unknown

CHAPTER FOUR
The Husband And The Wife

A fine wedding and marriage license do not make the marriage; it is the union of two hearts that welds husband and wife together.
—Rev. H. R. L. Sheppard

THUS FAR, WE have discussed marriage a great deal. The two key ingredients in marriage are the husband and the wife. It is pertinent at this stage to explore what the husband and the wife bring individually to the mystery called marriage.

Adam was the first man and the first husband. God created Adam in his own image and from the rib of Adam, Eve was made. This is how it all started:

So God created man in His own image ... male and female He created them. Then God blessed them and God said to them, Be fruitful and multiply; fill the earth and subdue it; have dominion over the fish of the sea, over the birds of the air, and over every living thing that moves on the earth. (Genesis 1:27–28)

The husband is generally accepted as the head of his family and has dominion over things. Some husbands insist on absolute authority, which often leads to problems in the marriage. Husbands claim their leadership role from the Epistle of Paul the Apostle to the Ephesians, where it is said the following:

> *For the husband is head of the wife, as also Christ is the head of the church; and He is the Savior of the body. Therefore, just as the church is subject to Christ, so let the wives be to their own husbands in everything.* (Ephesians 5:23–24)

Such powerful statements can get into the head of a man who loves power and domination. People sometimes tend to follow the first thing they read from the Bible, without understanding the full implications and without reading the following or corresponding verses or chapters to have the full impact and meaning of what they read. Can you imagine being a wife and living with a man that holds such an absolute view on authority as described above? Since every coin has two sides, let us review the other side of the coin and different perspective.

Different perspective

The quotation below further shows the imperativeness of having all the facts before reaching a decision. This is necessary for balance, clarity, and objectivity, which are important in a marital relationship.

Husbands, love your wives, just as Christ also loved the church and gave Himself for her, that He might sanctify and cleanse her with the washing of water by the word, that He might present her to Himself a glorious church, not having spot or wrinkle or any such thing, but that she should be holy and without blemish. So husbands ought to love their own wives as their own bodies; he who loves his wife loves himself. For no one ever hated his own flesh, but nourishes and cherishes it, just as the Lord does the church. For we are members of His body, of His flesh and of His bones. For this reason a man shall leave his father and mother and be joined to his wife, and the two shall become one flesh. This is a great mystery, but I speak concerning Christ and the church. Nevertheless let each one of you in particular so love his own wife as himself, and let the wife see that she respects her husband. (Ephesians 5:25–33)

Impact and implications

The impact and implications of this quotation are profound. I cannot imagine any husband who is now one flesh with his wife insisting on having absolute authority and dominion over her. Insisting on that means you may not love your wife or there may be the possibility of personality adjustment issues that require the assistance and intervention of a professional therapist. As a husband, you likely do not understand the concept of marriage, the full meaning of sharing innermost thoughts, feelings, and affections that characterize marriage.

LOVE AND MARRIAGE PERSPECTIVES

You are probably not following God's commandment to treat others the way you want to be treated—and not keeping in mind that the same measure you use will be measured back against you.

Could you imagine children raised in an environment where the husband is domineering? Children learn by observation, mimicking, and associative learning techniques. Children who grow up with dominating fathers have a high tendency to dominate their spouses.

Marriage is a process of learning and a process of give-and-take, wherein respect and affection are reciprocated. Anything less than that is one-sided and falls short of the true meaning of marriage. It is necessary for a husband who does not know how to manage his household to take an example from the following qualities found in I Timothy 3:2–5:

> *The husband of one wife, temperate, sober-minded, of good behavior, hospitable, able to teach; not given to wine, not violent, not greedy for money, but gentle, not quarrelsome, not covetous; one who rules his own house well, having his children in submission with all reverence, for if a man does not know how to run his own house, how will he take care of the church of God?*

Husband should see wife as a gift

It is worthwhile when the husband sees the wife as a gift to him, which she is. We tend to take care of our gifts. The husband should love the wife and not abuse the wife. The husband should see the wife as a companion and a helper, for God intended for wives to complement their husbands. A wife is a husband's significant other, his better half given to him as a gift from God to enjoy and live with. Ecclesiastes 9:9 states:

> *Live joyfully with the wife whom you love all the days of your vain life which He has given you under the sun, all your days of vanity; for that is your portion in life, and in the labor which you perform under the sun.*

A husband should understand that as the head of the household, he is to protect his wife and provide for her as they live together. The first Epistle of Peter clearly states:

> *Husbands, likewise, dwell with them with understanding, giving honor to the wife, as to the weaker vessel, and as being heirs together of the grace of life, that your prayers may not be hindered.* (I Peter 3:7)

It is also the duty of the husband to ensure that the relationship with his wife is peaceful, the flow of love enhanced and compassion and respect reigns in their household.

> *Finally, all of you be of one mind, having compassion for one another; love as brothers, be tenderhearted, be courteous; not returning evil for evil or reviling for reviling, but on the contrary blessing, knowing that you were called to this, that you may inherit a blessing.* (I Peter 3:8–9)

Husband's role in submission

Submission in marriage is always a hot potato when it comes up for discussion. This is because the issue of submission is sometimes misunderstood, depending on the background of the person you are discussing it with. Some husbands take the role of submission at face value, without actually understanding the fine print of submission.

The fine print of submission

It is appropriate to review the fine print of submission to give clarity to couples who may have misunderstood the meaning and the intended purpose of submission.

The word submission has a negative connotation, causing some people's jaws to drop and eyes to pop when discussing its relation to marriage. It does not matter if the husband or the wife is being talked about when the subject of submission is under discussion. It still conjures up negative images in most people's minds. Submission is viewed by some people as the wife bowing to the husband, slavery, and even abuse. Instead of equality between husband and wife, sharing of the thoughts, feelings, and emotions that characterize marriage, submission in some instances gives the impression of a superior talking to a subordinate. Since the husband is viewed as the head of the household, submission assumes that the husband is superior and the wife the subordinate in the marriage.

Background and circumstances of submission

At the time of Peter's writing, there was much persecution of Christians. In the midst of that persecution, Peter was encouraging Christians of his time to conduct themselves courageously for Christ. They would do so by following Christ's teachings, submitting to his will, hence servants submitting to their masters, citizens to government, wives to husbands, husbands to wives, and Christians to one another. Some people tend to read that passage of wives submitting to their husbands without actually knowing the background or the circumstances of that statement, especially the obligation of the husband in regard to submission.

Can a wife submit to her husband and still be respected?

Yes. Only a husband who lacks understanding will not respect his wife in the first place, submission or no submission. Spouses should keep in mind that submission is a two-way street and is reciprocal in marriage. Just as a wife submits to a husband, a husband submits to his wife. Technically, submission is an added ingredient in marriage, allowing husband and wife to trade love and respect for each other.

Before I even conceived of the idea of writing this book, I was talking with some colleagues of mine (three females and four males) in my office at lunchtime. The issue of submission came up for discussion. A female colleague said, "I am not going to be no man's towel for him to wipe his hands on me as he pleases in the name of submission." We all laughed at her statement. I explained how submission is mutual respect for each other, in that as the husband respects the wife, she submits to him. A husband should be like Christ by following his examples. She responded that she had no problem with that type of submission, the way I explained it. The understanding of the meaning and the connotation of submission actually depends on the people in that marriage. The closer they are to God in their marriage, the more meaning submission has to them.

Where in the Bible is submission discussed?

As far as I know, wives submitting to their husbands were mentioned in five areas in the Bible. For the purpose of this book, I will focus on three areas but will quote only one, for the one that I am going to cite is more extensive than the other two.

> *Wives, likewise, be submissive to your own husbands, that even if some do not obey the word, they, without a word,*

> *may be won by the conduct of their wives, when they observe your chaste conduct accompanied by fear. Do not let your adornment be merely outward—arranging the hair, wearing gold, or putting on fine apparel—rather let it be the hidden person of the heart, with the incorruptible beauty of a gentle and quiet spirit, which is very precious in the sight of God. For in this manner, in former times, the holy women who trusted in God also adorned themselves, being submissive to their own husbands, as Sarah obeyed Abraham, calling him lord, whose daughters you are if you do good and are not afraid with any terror. (I Peter 3:1-6)*

In Colossians 3:18 and Ephesians 5:22, mention was also made about wives submitting to their husbands. It should be noted that at the end of the verse about wives submitting to their husbands, the verse immediately following admonished husbands to love their wives. This reiterates the mutuality between love and submission. In other words, there is a strong propensity that the more the husband loves his wife, the more the wife submits to her husband. So love and submission go hand in hand. Now where is the wife in all of this? That is the subject of our next discussion.

How about the wife?

Much has been said about the husband, and I can understand anyone at this point asking, "How about the wife?" Let us review and explore that question. The wife is the other key ingredient in a marriage, the other half of one flesh that completes and complements the husband. Together they complete that mystery and puzzle called marriage. Despite the demise at the Garden of Eden, Proverbs 18:22 stated the following:

He who finds a good wife finds a good thing, and obtains favor from the Lord.

That shows the importance of a wife to mankind. A wife is a gift from God, and no amount of money can buy a good wife, as can be seen in Proverbs 19:14:

Houses and riches are an inheritance from fathers, but a prudent wife is from the Lord.

What are the qualities of a good wife?

What is a good wife? That depends on many factors. Defining a good wife is like defining beauty, in that they are both in the eye of the beholder. When a man is seeking a wife, he has certain attributes that he is looking for. Some men look for attractiveness. Attraction varies on an individual basis. For some men, that attraction could be the color of the hair, the height, the color of the skin, or the overall physical shape of the potential wife. Some men concentrate on what is on the inside, like the character of the woman, her personality, her relationship with God, and things of that nature. Some consider the woman's education, the type of job she has, her income potential, her ability to have children, and her family background. Those factors can either

THE HUSBAND AND THE WIFE

be endogenous or exogenous. The Bible states that a good wife possesses the qualities listed below:

> *That they admonish the young women to love their husbands, to love their children, to be discreet, chaste, homemakers, good, obedient to their own husbands, that the word of God may not be blasphemed.* (Titus 2:4–5)

As it did in the issue of submission, the Bible quickly and further admonished future husbands as follows:

> *Likewise, exhort the young men to be sober-minded, in all things showing yourself to be a pattern of good works; in doctrine showing integrity, reverence, incorruptibility, sound speech that cannot be condemned, that one who is an opponent may be ashamed, having nothing evil to say of you.* (Titus 2:6–8)

Where does all this lead us?

Marriage is not a battle of the sexes. It is a mutual understanding between spouses, where affections and emotions commingle. The most important thing is to remember that the wife is the husband, and the husband is the wife. They are one flesh by virtue of their marriage. They have gone through trials and tribulations together and have bonded as a result of that. Husband and wife are the same, in that both of them came from one God. The Bible made this more illustrative in 1 Corinthians 11:11:

Nevertheless, neither is man independent of woman, nor woman independent of man, in the Lord.

Husbands, wake up and smell the coffee

The future of marriage is changing. If the current trend continues in its present direction, the traditional roles of the husband and wife as we know them are outdated. I received my weekly subscription of *Time* magazine as I was writing this chapter. There was a special report titled "What Women Want Now," by Nancy Gibbs, hereinafter known as the *Time* study, which I feel warrants mentioning in this book. The reason for this is that some of the findings will have a profound effect on the trend and direction of roles in marriage.

The study (2009, 25) noted the following: "It's expected that by the end of the year, for the first time in history the majority of workers in the U.S. will be women — largely because the downturn has hit men so hard and more women are the primary breadwinner in their households almost 40% are providing essential income for the family's bottom line. Their buying power has never been greater — and their choices have seldom been harder."

This finding is consistent with Bengtson, Biblarz, and Roberts (2002, 164):

"Women's greater education and economic power within marriage may mean that they participate in household decision making about child rearing, consumption, and other life choices not only in their role as wives and mothers but as educational equals and breadwinners."

Changing gender roles

This section shows how women's gender roles have reversed in the thirty-seven-year span from 1972 to 2009. I will summarize some of the findings of the *Time* study and provide my personal statistical analysis of reversing gender roles:

(1) In 1972, only 7% of the students playing high school sports were girls; now the number is six times as high.

(2) The female dropout rate has fallen in half. College used to be almost 60/40 male; now the ratio has reversed, and close to half of law and medical degrees go to women, up from fewer than 10% in 1970.

(3) For the first time, five women have won Nobel prizes in the same year (for medicine, chemistry, economics, and literature).

(4) The current president of the United States (number forty-four) was raised by a single mother and married a lawyer who outranked and out earned him.

(5) Poll after poll finds women even more anxious than men about their family's financial security.

LOVE AND MARRIAGE PERSPECTIVES

(6.) Nearly half of women surveyed in households earning less than $75,000 want to delay pregnancy or limit the number of children they have.

(7) 65% of women reported being their family's chief financial planner, and 71% called themselves the family accountant. They also make 75% of the buying decisions in American homes.

(8) Together women control more wealth than ever in history.

(9) More than eight in ten say mothers are just as productive at work as fathers or childless workers are.

(10) 84% affirm that husbands and wives negotiate the rules, relationships, and responsibilities more than those of earlier generations did.

(11) Roughly seven in ten men say that they are more comfortable than their fathers were with women working outside the home, while women say they are less financially dependent on their spouses than their mothers were.

(12) The number of females in the following areas was zero prior to 1971, and the following are numbers in 2009 (words in parentheses are mine):

- Supreme Court justices: 2 (Actually, there have been three so far since 1971; the first appointee, Sandra Day O'Conner, retired.)

- Cabinet members: 7

- Avon executives (vice president or higher): 6

- Governors: 6

- FBI agents: 2,396

- Ivy League presidents: 4

(13) Among the most dramatic changes in the past generation is the detachment of marriage and motherhood; more men than women identified marriage as "very important to their happiness."

(14) Women no longer viewed matrimony as a necessary station on the road to financial security or parenthood.

(15) The percentage of children born to single women has leaped from 12% to 39%.

(16) Whereas a majority of children in the mid-1970s were raised by a stay-at-home parent, the portion is now less than a third, and nearly two-thirds of people say this has been a negative for American society.

(17) Among the most confounding changes of all is the evidence, tracked by numerous surveys, that as women have gained more freedom, more education, and more economic power, they have become less happy.

The last finding stated above is consistent with the Qian (1998, 279–92) hypothesis:

"Traditionally, women in the United States have married men who were better educated than themselves. Improvement in women's educational attainment over the past thirty years has, for the first time, reversed this trend. In fact, since 1986 marriages in which women were better educated than their husbands have become more likely than marriages in which men were better educated than their wives."

Statistical implications on husband/wife roles and impact on marriage

The *Time* study gave impressive statistical findings. I tend to analyze and expatiate further on issues concerning marriage and family. This attempt will aid in arriving at valid conclusions, inferences, and generalizations. In other words, I am giving more in-depth analyses with the intention of facilitating more understanding of the subject matter under reference. My analyses immediately follow each point below.

(A) The median age at which a woman got married for the first

THE HUSBAND AND THE WIFE

time in 1972 was twenty-one, and twenty-six is the median age at which women marry today for the first time.

This supports the conclusion that women married at a younger age in the past. One of the reasons is that in those days, the main role of women was homemaking, taking care of the needs of their husbands and children. They essentially worked at home full time. With the progression of time and the advent of women's liberation, the role of women in the family started changing, and more women started seeking work outside the home. As they became more career-oriented, women sometimes opted to delay marriage in order to secure a career.

(B) The number of children living with a single mother was 13% in 1972 and 23% in 2008.

More children living with a single mother could be explained through a high divorce rate. As divorce rates rise, so does the number of children living with a single parent. Most family courts have determined that children's best interests are served if they are placed with their mothers. Some mothers remain single by either design or other circumstances beyond their control. In addition, some women choose not to marry but to have children outside of marriage, as was the case with the fictional character Murphy Brown.

(C) Women age forty-five to fifty-four who never married: 5% in 1970 and 10% in 2008.

LOVE AND MARRIAGE PERSPECTIVES

Some women choose not to get married, likely because they haven't found a suitable mate or have delayed marriage for career. By the time they felt ready for marriage, they were past childbearing age or had advanced so much in their careers that potential mates were already taken. Either way, this group continues to grow. With the advent of alternative lifestyles, it may keep growing.

(D) Rate of divorce per one thousand persons was one in four 1972 and three in five in 2008.

This finding is surprising because most available literature supports the notion of an increasing divorce rate. What probably is happening is that as people cohabitate or enter into common-law marriages, those types of living arrangements are not registered or reported, and they are therefore not part of the statistical reports. Most people in common-law marriages do not even know they need to file for divorce at the end of that union. A common-law marriage is legal in most states so long as the two people (man and woman) involved present themselves together as husband and wife, live in the same house together, have a joint bank account, and file income tax returns together as spouses. When no divorce is filed for at the demise of this living arrangement, it may give the impression that the divorce rate is declining. Even in traditional marriages, some spouses never file for divorce in hopes of reconciliation, which doesn't usually happen. Some husbands in their quest to avoid paying child support leave the home, and never file for divorce; they return occasionally for sex but technically live with another woman in the same or different city. All these and other factors further lend credence to the fact that while nominally the divorce rate may be declining, in reality it is not.

(E) There are now 3.3 million married couples in which the wife is the sole earner. That is 2.4 million more than in 1970.

This shows that in the workforce, not only has the woman arrived, but she has taken over. This factor alone is the most dominant factor contributing to role reversal in marriage. More husbands stay at home and take care of the children. When I was in vocational rehabilitation counseling, a female consultant stated that her husband now stays at home due to her earning capacity, and he feels comfortable in his new role. They'd agreed that the one who made more money should go to work, and the other should stay at home. Both are happy with their decisions and roles in the family.

(F) In households where both partners have jobs, 55% of women and 28% of men agree that women take on more responsibilities of the home and family than their male partners do.

This is so because both have regular jobs, and when he gets home, the husband feels that he has done his traditional role, which is going to work outside the home. The wife, on the other hand, comes back from her own paid work and sees it as the starting of her traditional role in the house, which is to cook,

LOVE AND MARRIAGE PERSPECTIVES

take care of the children, and do other household chores. She still has to give the husband sex before sleeping at the end of all this work at home. Most wives complain that their husbands are not helping with chores at home and feel this as unfair. Hutter (1997, quoting Hochsheild, 1989, 245) noted as follows:

"Since 1980 women have taken 80% of the new jobs in the economy. Women's movement into the cash economy has drastically changed their lives. Yet at the same time, the traditional view that child rearing and housework are 'women's work' strongly persists.... While women have gone out to paid work most men have not increased their care of the home. But, perhaps even more important, men emotionally support this change in women far less than do women."

(G) About 71% of men are more comfortable than their fathers were with women working outside the home.

This seems understandable from men's point of view. At that garden called Eden, God gave man a woman as a helper, and some men perceive women working outside the home as a way of helping the husband and family. A more plausible explanation is that with the advancement of society, it is becoming difficult, if not impossible, for a family to survive on one paycheck, which traditionally came from the husband. It therefore became necessary for women to enter the workforce for the family to survive.

(H) Women describe their marriages as follows: 66% are very

happy; 30% pretty happy; 3% not too happy; and 1% not happy at all.

This finding is statistically even with men. It tends to solidify the notion that in marriage, happiness means different things for different people—that which equates to happiness for one couple may not be the same for another couple. Why is this so? First, people marry for different reasons and they get happy to the extent their objective in marriage is met. Some women may not completely happy due to emerging trends as their traditional roles are being challenged. Benard (1981, citing Gould, 1974, 98–99, and Komavovsky, 1940) notes the following:

"If she made a good salary, however, she is co-opting the man's passport to masculinity and he was effectively castrated. A wife's earning capacity diminished a man's position as the head of the household."

Failure in the role of good provider, which employment of wives evidenced, could produce deep frustration. Komarovsky (1940, 20) noted this about men:

"In his own estimation he is failing to fulfill what is the central duty of his life, the very touchstone of his manhood—the role of family provider."

(I) Approximately 70% say women are less financially dependent on their spouses than their mothers were.

LOVE AND MARRIAGE PERSPECTIVES

This is because women have made an appreciable impact on the workforce. It should be noted that women's earnings over the past decade have further increased. Income disparity between men and women further narrowed; such disparities are almost extinct at this time. Women continue to rise to top positions that were exclusively for men. That upward mobility in employment has catapulted women to the upper social strata, giving them tremendous purchasing power. This has given women unprecedented freedom; if the title of "head of household" is based on who brings home a bigger paycheck, household headship reverts to the women based on that criterion. The number of professional degrees awarded to women keeps increasing; so does the number of degrees in other areas awarded to women. This increase in the number of degrees awarded further results in increased paycheck for the women. If this continues to be the trend, the percentage of women who will be less dependent on their spouses will perhaps continue to rise.

(J) 52% of women and 27% of men strongly agree that women still bear the responsibility for taking care of sick or elderly parents.

This finding is consistent with the premise that women are more nurturing than men are. The logic to that premise is that God made women that way through childbirth—that every being nurtures its offspring. Add love to that equation, and the degree of nurturing increases, for people nurture what they care for and love.

THE HUSBAND AND THE WIFE

(K) 54% of women and 38% of men strongly agree that it is possible for a woman to have a fulfilling life if she remains single.

The quality of the life of women has increased considerably. Women are becoming more affluent than ever before. Some even delay pregnancy for careers. Some also choose not to marry. More women are acquiring skills needed to compete in today's world. With this affluence and these skills comes greater purchasing power than single women had about two decades ago, contributing to more fulfilling lives. One may want to argue that a woman who is single with all these attributes -- namely: money, power, skills, and freedom -- may be lacking sexual fulfillment since she is single. Think again, for a woman with all those attributes can easily get a man she desires for sexual fulfillment, without having to go through some of the frustrations of marriage.

(L) Which would you most want a daughter of yours to have—a happy marriage and children, financial success, or an interesting career?

It is important to state that every parent wants the best for his or her children, daughters inclusive. Women most often choose financial success and an interesting career for their daughters, just as they themselves are more career-oriented than they were in traditional marriages decades ago. On the other hand, men choose happy marriage and children. The rationale could stem from the fact that men continue to value marriage in the

LOVE AND MARRIAGE PERSPECTIVES

traditional way, where a man cares for and protects the wife. That care and protection translates into how good a provider the man is. The men's reasoning could also be that regardless of the outcome of the daughter's situation financially or in relation to her career, her husband would take care of her at the end of the day. Alternatively, women might reason that with financial success and an interesting career, her daughter can take care of herself and her children, regardless of the outcome in the marriage. If this continues to be the trend in marriage, the traditional marriage as we know it may be outdated.

(M) 85% of women and 79% of men agree that it is now more acceptable for men to be stay-at-home dads than it was in the previous generations.

This type of arrangement would have been unheard of two or three decades ago. Even if such an arrangement or agreement existed then, it would not have been acceptable to the degree it is today. It would have been a slap in the face for a man to stay home and do household chores like cooking, cleaning, child rearing, and so on. The core of his manhood would have been in question if he stayed at home and his wife went to work to be the breadwinner for the family. This shows the changing nature of the marriage institution—and how present-day marriage is being impacted.

(N) Men and women were given the following seven issues and told to select which were most important to them: being healthy, being self-sufficient, being financially secure, having a fulfilling job, having religious faith, having children, and being married.

Having a fulfilling job was statistical dead heat, with women at 72% and men at 73%. Men came out on top as far as being married, with 58% as opposed to 53% for women. Women polled higher in other areas mentioned above. This may even pose another question regarding marriage. With all these statistical findings, who actually controls the present-day marriage? Is it the man or woman? This explanation may establish a not-so-surprising cause-and-effect relationship between power and control in a marriage relative to gender roles.

(O) All things considered, men continue to have it better in life than women do—23% of women and 12% of men agreed.

Looking at this from a woman's perspective, yes, men have it better in life than a woman. Why? Let us look at men and women in marriage. Women are more likely to do more household chores than men are. The burden of child care typically falls to the woman rather than the man. Men are more likely to get out of the home to hang out with their friends on weekends while the women are stuck at home babysitting or doing laundry or other chores in the house. More men have recreational memberships to golf clubs, football associations, basketball tournaments, and things of that sort. These issues definitely have affected today's marriage.

(P) You are comfortable with the woman in the household earning more money than the man—89% of women and 89% of men agree.

You do not have to be a rocket scientist to figure this out. Husbands and wives do not seem to care who makes more money, so long as that money is seen as their money collectively, in a joint or even in a separate account. Problems sometimes arise when one spouse, especially a woman, gets her paycheck but refuses to contribute to anything toward the upkeep of the family. The woman who is refusing to contribute takes the notion that the man is the provider and as such should take full responsibility for household expenses. This statistical dead even is so in that couples in the household want their bills paid in time to protect their credit. When a marriage is at a harmonious stage, it does not seem to matter to either spouse who brings in more money, for they still subscribe to the theory of one flesh in marriage. When either person starts withholding some of his or her money for motives that have nothing to do with the betterment of the marriage, this may be of some concern because it appears to be the beginning of a structural weakness in that marriage which may ultimately result in its demise.

And so what?

One may be wondering why this heading is titled "And so what?" This is so in that Matthew 16:26 asks the following:

THE HUSBAND AND THE WIFE

What does it profit a man if he gains the world but loses his soul?

We are talking about the unprecedented wealth that women have acquired and the impact of their purchasing power. Remember that sometimes money is not everything. I am not against two wage earners in the family, but here are some things that we may want to ponder or consider. Motherhood is a calling. No career can compete with motherhood, and I applaud women who try to juggle both careers. I believe in balancing things in life. Still, a woman should not allow her primary role as wife and mother to be superseded by other issues, interests, or responsibilities. This individual decision will vary from family to family. While a career is often necessary, it can sometimes be delayed in the interest of the family and the children.

These bills have to be paid, and in the process of paying those bills, we should not let the money we make go to our heads. Remember that God provided us with that money. The money we make comes with certain obligations, such as tithes. Malachi 3:8 reads as follows:

> "Will a man rob God? Yet you have robbed Me! But you say, 'In what have we robbed You?' In tithes and offerings."

As you can see, this obligation is stated in plain language for all to understand. God is the last one we would like to rob. I am not insinuating that we have robbed anybody, but the scriptural

LOVE AND MARRIAGE PERSPECTIVES

significance is that the same way God gives, the same way he can take. As spouses and parents, we have to be in a good relationship with God. We have to ask for his blessings and guidance so that he can protect us and our children. Sometimes we receive our blessings and do not even know it. Our jobs our paychecks are blessings from God.

I remember listening to my parents' music collection when I was little. One song that caught my attention was by a musician named Jim Reeves. The first part of the song goes like this: *This world is not my home and I am just passing through. My treasures are laid up somewhere beyond the blue. The angels beckon me from heaven's open door, and I don't feel at home in this world anymore.* This can relate to Matthew 6:19:

> *For where your treasure is there your heart will be also.*

So as we make that money and build up our nest eggs and treasures, we should not forget where our real treasures should be. Our decision is what takes priority: worldly treasure or eternal treasure with God? It is further stated in Matthew 18:18 that "Assuredly, I say to you, whatever you bind on earth will be bound in heaven, and whatever you loose on earth will be loosed in heaven." I am not advocating that you should not go to work and provide for your family. I am just saying not to leave God out in doing so. God helps those who help themselves. Even at your lowest ebb, when you do not have, God will provide for you the same way he provided for the birds of the air. We are assured of this in Matthew 6:25–26:

THE HUSBAND AND THE WIFE

Therefore I say to you, do not worry about your life, what you will eat or what you will drink; nor about your body, what you will put on. Is not life more than food and the body more than clothing? Look at the birds of the air, for they neither sow nor reap nor gather into barns; yet your heavenly Father feeds them. Are you not of more value than they?

By the same line of reasoning, as you make your money, eat, and are satisfied and merry, keep God in your daily affairs. Make God your priority, as it is written in Matthew 4:14:

Man shall not live by bread alone but by every word that proceeds from the mouth of God.

So do not forget God in your quest for your riches. If you humble yourself before God, that will be a wise move, for Proverbs states that before honor is humility. Matthew 23:12 states:

Whoever exalts himself shall be humbled.

Finally, in Matthew 19:23–24, it is written:

Then Jesus said to His disciples, Assuredly, I say to you that it is hard for a rich man to enter the kingdom of heaven. And again I say to you, it is easier for a camel to go through the eyes of a needle than for a rich man to enter the kingdom of God.

LOVE AND MARRIAGE PERSPECTIVES

In closing, this chapter is not advocating that you shun riches—you should not. God created things in this world for us to enjoy, and money is one such thing. However, in seeking those riches, we should strive to strike a balance whereby we make an effective contribution to things that affect us, like our spouses, children, careers, daily lives, and God.

When a man brings his wife flowers for no reason, there is a reason.

—Molly McGee

CHAPTER FIVE

The Family—Customs, Traditions, And Roles

In every conceivable manner, the family is the link to our past, bridge to our future.

—Alex Haley

THE FAMILY IS an agency of socialization. In marriage, husbands and wives are responsible for building rapport and interaction in the marriage. In Christian culture, the family has a unique representation. In this instance, the family is seen as a chosen instrument of God for reproduction, as Adam was advised in Genesis to "be fruitful and multiply." Some versions of the Bible have it as "increase and multiply." As children become part of the family, it is expected that they will be nurtured in the process. Moral principles will be propagated so that they can follow the will of God and teach the same to their own children. The family, like any other institution, appears to be going through some transformation, and if the trend continues, it may have a pervasive effect on the structure of the family. The nuclear family is in decline, but before we look into why, let us attempt to define what a nuclear family is.

Definition of a nuclear family

Several authors have attempted to define a nuclear or traditional family. For the purposes of this book, the best definition that I have found so far is the one by Popenoe (1990, 39–51), which stated the following:

"A nuclear family is a family situated apart from both the larger kin group and workplace; focused on the procreation of children; and consisting of a legal, lifelong, sexually exclusive, heterosexual, monogamous marriage, based on affection and companionship, in which there is a sharp division of labor, with the female as full-time housewife and the male as primary provider and ultimate authority."

In the past, our ancestors witnessed an era of high marriage rates, with more emphasis on having children. It is pertinent to state that traditional nuclear families were strong back then, and children were growing up in homes where both parents were present. With the passing of time, however, the number of traditional families started declining. Now let us review some of the factors that were responsible for the decline of traditional family.

Children no longer a priority

Procreation has been one of the cardinal functions of the family. This traditional function of the family started becoming less prominent as having children no longer became the priority

THE FAMILY—CUSTOMS, TRADITIONS, AND ROLES

that it once was. Gone were the days of the pride, success, or the wealth of the family depending on the number of children a family had. Having children no longer wielded the influence and status symbols that it once did. In fact, according to society and culture, having fewer children became the order of the day. People started looking at families with many children as being out of tune with reality. Even the stigma associated with barrenness and childlessness disappeared completely.

The workforce

An unprecedented number of women entered the workforce. The traditional role of a woman staying at home taking care of the children, husband, and other domestic chores became an illusion. Bengtson, Biblarz, and Roberts (2002, 33), quoting the U.S. Bureau of Labor Statistics (1999) noted the following:

"A major social trend affecting families over the past decades has been the steady increase of women in the paid labor force. In a pattern mirroring the trend for divorce, the mothers of generation X were more than twice as likely as mothers of baby boomers to have participated in paid labor force."

It became almost insulting to advise a woman to stay at home and not enter the workforce. As more women joined the job market, traditional roles that were exclusively women's became a joint responsibility of the husband and wife. Day cares started to spring up to care for children whose mothers joined the workforce. The traditional family was never the same since then. Remember that with the mother in the workforce, the child is at a day care center. These workers and children do not have the type of emotional bonding as the children have with their mothers. This lack of emotional connection or bonding probably affects the child's developmental growth.

Increased divorce rate

The resultant effect was that divorce, which was unheard of in traditional families, reared its ugly head. With the progression of time, the divorce rate shot through the roof. In one study, Glick (1988, 868) noted:

"The year 1974 was a landmark, in that for the first time in American history, more marriages ended in divorce than in death."

What are the effects of these changes on the family?

The concomitant effect of all these changes is the dissipation of the traditional family because of a weakened structure. This has had a far-reaching effect on husband and wife in that the traditional bonding and nucleus of the family has lost ground to single-parent households and stepfamilies. The profound and far-reaching effect this had on family and children is difficult to reverse. This not only changed the family structure but also the psychological character of marital relationships. Remember that marriage is a union of two personalities, but even as they

THE FAMILY—CUSTOMS, TRADITIONS, AND ROLES

become one flesh, they are still two distinct personalities. The trends that the traditional family is undergoing have changed the experiences and connections to the institution of family.

There is an argument in some quarters that there is no more institution in the family, prompting another argument that even the institution of marriage is deinstitutionalized. As the norms and mores of a traditional marriage are diluted, so are the norms of a traditional family structure. It is then safe to establish a correlation between deterioration of family and deterioration of marriage, in that both go hand in hand. Certain sets of norms and obligations that were widely enforced and expected in traditional marriage are now outdated. With this new emerging trend, some people do not even take their vows seriously. Most traditional things done in the marriage today in regards to vows are voluntary, especially for those who love their spouses. Such is also the state of affairs in today's family structure. The only thing that may still be enforceable is the child support, and that depends on whether the spouse paying child support has a job so that wages can be garnished.

An ethos has definitely emerged, and with this emergence comes a new order. What this new order will be depends on time, and the direction of this new ethos. Regardless of the direction, the clear-cut conclusion is that traditional family is declining. It is important to review the implications of this decline.

LOVE AND MARRIAGE PERSPECTIVES

Decline of nuclear family

Several positions have been stated in regard to decline or purported decline of the traditional family. Some schools of thought are of the opinion that the traditional family is weakening; others believe the traditional family is declining. Regardless of whatever position or notion you subscribe to, it is undeniable that the traditional family has lost its cohesiveness. This decline, some argue, is positive because the fact of more women entering the workforce has brought an unprecedented amount of wealth to the family structure. The same line of reasoning emphasizes the emancipation of women in that they are no longer tied to the home and the kitchen because of the changing gender roles.

Children are the ones impacted negatively by the decline of traditional family. Take into consideration that what impacts children today impacts the future generation of tomorrow. Does this mean that we can sacrifice our children at the expense of wealth? Do not get me wrong; I am not against paying bills and bringing additional income to the family. The question here is whether we can find a better way of seeking that income or balance without putting the children in such a precarious situation. Can't we find a better way to preserve the traditional family?

This rush to unprecedented wealth at the expense of the family has another undesirable effect on the family as well: it breeds absentee fathers in some families where disparity in income may prompt a husband who is uncomfortable about his wife

THE FAMILY—CUSTOMS, TRADITIONS, AND ROLES

making more money than him. This absenteeism further shatters the structure and cohesiveness of the traditional family and the loss of a good provider role in the family. The unprecedented wealth that would have resulted from the combined income of both parents becomes illusory when the father is absent from the home. Lack of a consistent relationship between a father and his children is also hurtful. Children experience additional trauma as they shuttle from one home to another, between their father and mother. Historically, maternal child rearing under these circumstances has become more difficult and even problematic.

The resultant effect of this decline in traditional families is that fewer people are marrying, and the ones that choose to marry are doing so later in life. Marriages are resulting in fewer children. Divorce is decimating the marriages, in that more couples are divorcing. Take into account that some couples may disagree on some issues, separate, and never get divorced—but live with a different partner. The family also has a shorter life span, and the people in it face an uncertain future due to these instabilities and the decline in the traditional family. The impact of all the mentioned effects has a devastating and profound effect on the family as whole.

Impact on family

The institution of family is going through some metamorphoses, and a new order appears to be emerging. The ethos and characteristics of this new order seem to be taking root in issues emerging in present-day families, and may likely be the pattern of future families. Debates are quietly emerging, and some are suggesting that the institution of family has been dying for about two decades now because of the metamorphosis that the family is undergoing. One school of thought is that the family is not dying but is in a state of decay, and if nothing is done to reverse the trend, then that will spell the beginning of death for the family as we know it. The other school of thought is that the institution of family, for all practical purposes, is already dead, and subsequent efforts have shown our inability as a society to restore vitality to a diseased organ.

Regardless of which notion or theory you subscribe to, two things are perfectly clear: one, the institution of family is no longer traditional as we knew it; two, family structures have fluctuated considerably in the past thirty or forty years.

Couples are deliberately postponing having children, and if they finally decide to have them, the number of children is few. Some have even chosen to be childless, probably for career issues or other reasons. A great majority of the reasoning for not having children is purely voluntary and individualistic.

It is imperative to state that as new family patterns are emerging, so are marriage patterns. These emerging patterns have profound implications for the family. Couples are choosing cohabitation in place of marriage and are having children while doing so. As the cohabitating couples in most cases decide to dissolve their relationships, go their separate ways, and end up cohabitating with

THE FAMILY—CUSTOMS, TRADITIONS, AND ROLES

new individuals, can you imagine the fate of the children born during the first cohabitation? Questions emerge as to the following: how to enforce child support collection? The father may argue that he is not the father—perhaps because no record of a marriage existed, and in most instances, acknowledgment of paternity is not signed in this type of living arrangement. In addition, in the new cohabiting arrangement, is the new man the stepfather? Another issue in this new cohabitation arrangement -- whose last name will the child have? Is it the father's or the mother's? Take into account that no marriage existed in the first place—or does cohabitating qualify a common-law marriage, depending on the state where they live? There are many more questions than answers, and all these impact the family.

Women appear to the ones impacted most by these emerging patterns. What of women who never marry but continue to have illegitimate children? When I was in chemical dependency counseling, there was a woman who had six children. The children had different last names, as they were given their fathers' last names. Single motherhood appears to be on a steady rise. Women continue to make major advances in the workforce, and the increase in day care centers continues to keep pace with the birth rate. More mothers are juggling careers and child rearing, and they appear to be excelling at both.

Divorce rates that were steadily rising appear to be tapering off, at least in the opinion of one study. Nevertheless, divorce and divorce rates continue to impact families negatively.

LOVE AND MARRIAGE PERSPECTIVES

However, one pattern that emerged is the greater involvement of men in household chores, especially where both couples work outside the home. Men's issues have not been in the forefront as much as women's issues, or perhaps not as much controversy has been generated in this area. Regardless of the generation of issues or the lack of them, gender roles continue to change and reverse as patterns of families continue to emerge. Scanzoni (1975, 38) noted: "Possibility of a different pattern in which the responsibility for households would unequivocally fall equally on husbands as well as wives."

The findings of other studies continue to support this position. Hall and Hall (1979), in their study of two-career couples, learned the following: "Most serious fights among such couples occur not in the bedroom but in the kitchen, between couples who profess a commitment of equality, but who find actually implementing it difficult."

Past and current studies continue to emphasize equality as far as household chores. At this stage of family metamorphosis, some patterns of the future of the family in America continue to emerge. It seems safe to conclude that with these evolving and emergent patterns, no distinctive pattern appears to be predominant. As all these changes, controversies, and debates rage on, the future of the family will hopefully transform in such a way that it will not have a deleterious effect on marriage and family relations in America.

THE FAMILY—CUSTOMS, TRADITIONS, AND ROLES

God's intention

God's intention is for the family to be in harmony, with husband and wife multiplying and raising their children to understand and love God just as Christ Jesus loved the children. Jesus demonstrated his love for children when the children were brought to him and the disciples rebuked them. The children were brought to him so he might lay his hands on them and pray. Consider these words from Matthew 19:14–15:

> *Jesus said, "Let the little children come to Me, and do not forbid them; for of such is the kingdom of heaven." And he laid His hands on them and departed from there.*

As parents, it is our responsibility to bring our children close to God. That cannot happen unless we lead the way and our children follow our example. Children may not be able to understand God unless we teach them. As parents, we fail in our obligation when we do not teach our children to have a relationship with God. I will be quoting extensively from the Gospel according to Matthew, and the reader of this book may want to know why. The reason is that all the synoptic Gospels are essentially identical narrative about the life of Jesus Christ, and as I write, I have the Gospel of Matthew in front of me for ease of reference. Continuing with my argument about teaching our children the right and wrong way, as parents we are the guide of our children. In Matthew 5:13, it is stated:

LOVE AND MARRIAGE PERSPECTIVES

You are the salt of the earth; but if the salt loses its flavor, how shall it be seasoned? It is then good for nothing but to be thrown out and trampled underfoot by men.

The question is, if the salt loses its flavor, how shall it be seasoned? Let me pose the meaning of that question in regard to children and the family. If we as parents fail to teach our children the way of God, what kind of children will they be when they are grown? Let us take this even further. Can you imagine how their children will turn out when they grow up? I do not see any good scenarios with the answers. The family is the foundation for the child, and when the family does not give the child a good foundation, that child is lost. It is like the foolish Biblical man who built his house on sand:

But everyone who hears these sayings of Mine, and does not do them, will be like a foolish man who built his house on the sand: and the rain descended, the floods came, and the winds blew and beat on that house; and it fell. And great was its fall. (Matthew 7:26–27)

Jesus shows abundant love to children

Jesus has demonstrated his abundant love to children. All we have to do as parents is guide and direct the children to him. Ponder this passage:

How often I wanted to gather your children together, as the hen gathers her chicks under her wings, but you were

THE FAMILY—CUSTOMS, TRADITIONS, AND ROLES

not willing! See! Your house is left to you desolate; for I say to you, you shall see me no more till you say, "Blessed is He who comes in the name of the Lord." (Matthew 23:37–39)

It is incumbent on us as parents to turn our children to God so that they can follow his ways. In demonstrating his love for children, Jesus assured us that whoever receives just one child in his name receives him. What a pinnacle of demonstration of love for children. That illustration is clear in Matthew 18:3–5:

Assuredly, I say to you, unless you are converted and become as little children, you will by no means enter the kingdom of heaven. Therefore whoever humbles himself as this little child is the greatest in the kingdom of heaven. Whoever receives one little child like this in My name receives Me.

He continued by reiterating his love for children when he said later in Matthew 18:10–11:

Take heed that you do not despise one of these little ones, for I say to you that in heaven their angels always see the face of My Father who is in heaven. For the Son of Man has come to save that which was lost.

He wants us to love our children the same way he loves them. In Matthew 7:9–11, he asked as follows:

Or what man is there among you who, if his son asks for

> *bread, will give him a stone? Or if he asks for a fish, will he give him a serpent? If you then, being evil, know how to give good gifts to your children, how much more will your Father who is in heaven give good things to those who ask Him!*

We should love our children in such a way as not to spoil them. One way of loving and not spoiling is to teach children in the process of loving them. In Matthew 7:24, it was equated to a wise man who built his house on a rock:

> *Therefore whoever hears these sayings of Mine, and does them, I will liken him to a wise man who built his house on the rock.*

And in Matthew 5:19:

> *But whoever does and teaches them, he shall be called great in the kingdom of heaven.*

Bear in mind that as we teach our children, they learn by observing. They will accomplish fellowship with Jesus and, as stated in Matthew 15:4–6, have the greatest respect a child can have for his parents:

> *For God commanded, saying, "Honor your father and your mother"; and, 'He who curses father or mother, let him be put to death. But you say, 'Whoever says to his father or mother, 'Whatever profit you might have received from*

me is a gift to God'—then he need not honor his father or mother.' Thus you have made the commandment of God of no effect by your tradition.

In closing, "let him be put to death" is a point worthy of clarification. This is meant to illustrate the seriousness of children honoring their parents, as no child should be put in harm's way. I needed to clarify that for the purposes of this book.

Comparative analysis

Another reason that Matthew was quoted exclusively in the preceding paragraphs was to make three distinct points. First, that Biblical literature is unanimous in stressing that God loves children abundantly and unequivocally. Second, that parents teaching and directing children is universal in Biblical literature. Third, those children are the future, and if we do not hand over the baton of righteousness, the family as an agent of socialization has failed woefully.

Now let us review other Biblical writings on the children, and how they impact the family. In the book of Psalms, it talks about the children being a heritage as follows:

Behold, children are a heritage from the Lord. The fruit of the womb is a reward. Like arrows in the hands of a warrior, so are the children of one's youth. Happy is the man who has his quiver full of them; they shall not be ashamed,

> but shall speak with their enemies in the gate. (Psalm 127:3-5)

Children were presented in such a poetic prose, and as parents, we may be happy having a full house of them, but it is still our responsibility to let the children understand that they are heritage from the Lord. Fathers were given their charge concerning their children. Part of that charge included:

> And you, fathers, do not provoke your children to wrath, but bring them up in the training and admonition of the Lord. (Ephesians 6:4)

Including the above, there are also other duties, obligations, and responsibilities expected of fathers. Suffice it to say that mothers are also part of all these, in that training and guiding children is a joint responsibility.

You may be thinking that the children were left out of those responsibilities. No, they were not, in that they have their own cardinal charge:

> Children, obey your parents in the Lord. For this is right. (Ephesians 6:1)

You may have observed that this obedience is termed "right" per the quotation above -- why is it so? As children learn how to obey the Lord, they also learn how to obey their parents. As you

THE FAMILY—CUSTOMS, TRADITIONS, AND ROLES

obey your parents, you listen actively to what they are telling or advising you. Taking that advice enhances a cordial environment of leaning, which facilitates children being led to the path of God. In the process of learning, children ask questions. It is our responsibility as parents to answer their questions as objectively as possible, without twisting the facts to suit our purpose or objective. Ponder this:

> Then he spoke to the children of Israel, saying: "When your children ask their fathers in time to come, saying, 'What are these stones?' then you shall let your children know, saying, 'Israel crossed over this Jordan on dry land'; for the Lord your God did to the Red Sea, which He dried up before us until we had crossed over that all the peoples of the earth may know the hand of the Lord, that it is mighty, that you may fear the Lord your God forever." (Joshua 4:21–24)

When parents do not teach their children about the ways of the Lord, vital information that is passed on from generations will be lost. This unpassed information no doubt affects the family negatively. This issue is vividly illustrated in Judges:

> When all that generation had been gathered to their fathers, another generation arose after them who did not know the Lord nor the work which he had done for Israel. (Judges 2:10)

In closing, it is pertinent to state that the way we train our

LOVE AND MARRIAGE PERSPECTIVES

children or impart the knowledge enhances how the children can understand it. In Deuteronomy 6:4–9, a teaching procedure known as associative learning was used:

> *Hear, O Israel: the Lord our God, the Lord is one! You shall love the Lord your God with all your heart, with all your soul, and with all your strength. And these words which I command you today shall be in your heart. You shall teach them diligently to your children, and shall talk of them when you sit in your house, when you walk by the way, when you lie down, and when you rise up. You shall bind them as a sign on your hand, and they shall be as frontlets between your eyes. You shall write them on the doorposts of your house and on your gates.*

The love of a family is life's greatest blessing.
—Unknown

CHAPTER SIX

Communication Styles In Marriages

We have two ears and one mouth so that we can listen twice as much as we speak.
—Epictetus, Greek philosopher

IMAGINE TWO INDIVIDUALS who have never seen each other before meeting on the street. Put them in one room together for one day with no discussion whatsoever. At the end of the one-day exercise, ask them to write a ten-page comprehensive narrative about each other. I doubt if they can write more than one page, since they had no communication. That is what it is like when you and your spouse do not communicate. You live in one house together, but know absolutely nothing about each other. Communication is an essential ingredient that makes marriage work.

Why is communication important?

(A) It helps partners talk issues out.

(B) It helps explore feelings.

(C) Communication fosters closeness.

LOVE AND MARRIAGE PERSPECTIVES

(D) It breeds understanding.

(E) Communication is a key ingredient that helps build goals, values, and dreams in a relationship.

(F) It helps meet our needs.

(G) It prevents conflict by fostering understanding, and when a conflict arises, it helps to resolve it.

Communication is the life-wire of a marriage. The presence or lack of communication can make or break a marriage. Communication, or open dialogue, is one of the important -- if not the most important -- factors for a continuous marriage. The reason I refer to communication in marriage as an open dialogue is that marriage communication is different from other communication because in marriage you communicate with your heart and soul. Your emotion defines your communication in marriage. You do not want to leave any room for ambiguity. You want to make sure that your spouse understands what you are telling him or her. There is no guessing or second-guessing while communicating in marriage, which is why the communicator communicates with clarity and an open heart. Your spouse is your other half and you do not want to withhold any issue while communicating with him or her.

This type of communication is what I call body-to-body communication. The reason for that terminology is that you communicate with your whole body. Your spouse listens with his or her whole body. The spouse sending a message has the whole body talking by maintaining eye contact as he or she talks. The ear is also listening for any interjections while the person is talking. There are other subtle messages of love that the whole body emits and exhibits during this type of exchange. The receiver of the message also listens with his or her whole body through active listening. Active listening is where you give your spouse undivided attention by listening actively and attentively with your whole body: ears, eyes, hand gestures, nodding, and other nonverbal communicative skills. Chapman (2005) described this as empathetic listening and identified fourteen areas of empathetic listening.

ADVANTAGES OF BODY-TO-BODY COMMUNICATION

Attention

The first obvious advantage is that you communicate attentively, and your spouse listens attentively. With that type of focus and intense involvement while communicating, messages are sent and received with clarity.

Cordial environment

This type of communication enhances a cordial environment that is conducive for exchanging of ideas in a true give-and-take situation. The exchange is orderly. There is usually no type of argument in this kind of interaction.

Meeting objective

The objective of body-to-body communication is always met. That objective is meaningful interaction with the intention of resolving any marital problems. Another objective is fostering unity in marriage because of resolution of any issues or problems in the marriage.

Growth in marriage

The continuum of marriage is greatly enhanced because couples that have a mechanism in place to foster communication have a greater tendency or likelihood of injecting vitality in their marriage because of that built-in mechanism in the system.

Conflict resolution

The marriage has less conflict when there is body-to-body communication because issues are talked out in the process of open dialogue. The active listening mode helps resolution of issues before they escalate to conflict. Even when conflict arises, a mechanism of resolving issues is already in place through body-to-body communication.

Fostering intimacy

This communicative pattern fosters intimacy and closeness in that the couple is immersed in the body-to-body communicative system. They talk from the heart and listen from the heart. Their emotions, thoughts, feelings, and the future of their marriage are invested in this type of communication because it encompasses their entire bodies.

Win-win situation

Both people are happy at the end of this exchange because they get what they wanted, which is what triggers happiness. Resolution in marriage should not come to the point where one person lost and the other person won. For a resolution to be conclusive and definitive in marriage, each spouse has to feel a sense of accomplishment and resolution on an outcome that satisfies each spouse.

Understanding

The couple tends to understand each other more because this system fosters understanding due to the unique way it involves emotions. It further unites the hearts through the meeting or coming together of minds and souls due to deep sharing and exchange of ideas and dialogue. I will wrap up this section with two quotations from the book of Proverbs regarding active listening or body-to-body communication, and what one will gain as a result:

> *A wise man will hear and increase learning, And a man of understanding will attain wise counsel.* (Proverbs 1:5)

LOVE AND MARRIAGE PERSPECTIVES

Happy is the man who finds wisdom, and the man who gains understanding. (Proverbs 3:13)

Factors inhibiting marital communication

As I stated previously, marital communication is different from other communications because of the emotion involved in such communication. Let us review some obstacles, barriers, or factors negating effective marital communication.

Premature conclusions

Have you ever noticed the effect when two people are engaged in a conversation? The listener keeps interjecting to make his or her point instead of listening first, to be able to give an informed feedback. Imagine that in a marriage situation, where thoughts, and emotions come into play. The point of this scenario is that in marital communication, spouses are even more eager to interject, as each spouse wants to get his or her point across. The exception to this is the couple that has a more disciplined approach to communication or has skills like body-to-body or empathetic listening.

Can you further imagine giving a verdict on an issue about which you have no clue? Let me make this point more practicable and illustrative. Say that you are in a civil courtroom. The judge comes in, and the bailiff says, "All rise. This court is now in session, and the Honorable Judge Mr. Clueless is presiding."

The judge asks the clerk which case is first on the docket and wants the two litigants to please step forward. Without listening to any legal arguments, he reaches for a coin in his desk, points to the litigant on his right, and says, "Heads you win; tails you lose." The judge flips the coin, and lo and behold, the coin lands on tails. He tells that litigant that he lost his case. The judge closes the proceedings by adding that that is the verdict of the court, and so shall it be recorded and certified. That is similar to what happens when couples do not listen actively to each other by interjecting or not having a full and absolute grasp of the subject matter before reaching a conclusion or forming an opinion on an issue. Any opinion or conclusion in those instances is premature.

Flawed reasoning

This is concomitant to the point illustrated above, in that when a spouse does not have complete information, his or her reasoning is flawed. That couple's logic is not sequential, and with no sequentialism, his or her assertions, abstractions, conclusions, opinions, view, comments, reasoning, and logic are therefore flawed.

Incomplete information

This area shows the cause-and-effect relationship between lack of effective communication and lack of complete information. In other words, the incompleteness of your information or data translates to the incompleteness of the message you're sending to or receiving from your spouse.

Irrational expression

Uncertainty characterizes marital discord. Throw in the emotion involved in marital communication, especially when conflicting issues or incomplete information are involved because of inactive listening, and the result is irrationality of expression. Skills enumerated in body-to-body techniques or empathetic listening can help alleviate this communicative barrier.

Probable outcome

The possibility is that an unfavorable outcome may inhibit marital communication by discouraging one spouse from communicating effectively with the other. This is because the spouse sending a message may not articulate fully because of the concern that the other spouse may receive his or her message negatively.

Fear of rejection

A spouse may not communicate fully or openly because of the inherent fear in his or her mind of probable rejection if everything is disclosed. The spouse who wants to disclose but has this fear of rejection may be testing the limits and the timing of the disclosure. When gripped with fear, my rule of thumb in this type of disclosure is to consider the following:

(1) The stage of the marriage at the time of the disclosure. In other words, if trust is present and marital harmony is in place

that might be a fairly good time to disclose.

(2) The way the information is disclosed. Holding hands while disclosing and presenting the information in a cordial, respectful manner may be prudent.

(3) The timing of the disclosure. This includes the environment of the disclosure. A romantic environment is suggested. The mood and objectivity of each spouse at the time of the disclosure should be taken into account.

(4) The spouse receiving the disclosure should be considerate and supportive because the spouse disclosing is doing so out of love and in the interest of the marriage. The action of the receiving spouse, if not supportive and understanding, can freeze that disclosure.

Lack of trust

A marriage that lacks trust is like a car running on a racetrack with no driver. It is only a matter of time before that car crashes. Trust is a key element in marriage, and where trust is lacking, the marriage is like a house with no foundation. With no trust, there is no marriage, and with no marriage, there is basically nothing to communicate.

Withholding issues

Withholding in a marriage is like only part of you is married. Withholding by not sharing your feelings, intentions, thoughts, and perceptions robs you of the rewards and enrichment of marriage. A marriage is on life support when spouses are withholding issues from each other. Marital communication in those circumstances is rather forced. At best, communication can be described as a pack of lies. With lies in a marriage, the relationship is like the proverbial mustard seed in the Bible, for it too will likely wither away.

Ulterior motive

Some couples may have other motives as to why they are not communicating in marriage. Regardless of the situation, such ulterior motives are not in the best interest of the marriage and not fair to your spouse. What happened to the golden rule of treating others the way we want to be treated?

Fear of reprisal

The ability to talk freely with your spouse with great understanding and without repercussions ensures vitality in a marriage. Consequently, failure to communicate in a marriage is tantamount to failure of the marriage. When a husband and wife fail to understand each other, because communication is lacking or virtually nonexistent, the marriage is at a stagnant stage. The resultant effect is that the marriage turns into a meaningless nothingness, where the couple are no longer on the same page so to speak. Things then fall apart because the center of the marriage no longer holds. If this situation of affairs is not remedied, whether by mutual agreement of the couple or through external intervention such as professional counseling, the seed of discord will have been sown. If effective communication continues to elude the marriage, the bond of that marriage begins to break. The glue that held the marriage together starts separating. It is then a matter of time before the whole structure of that marriage completely crumbles and collapses.

We are never too old or too young to learn how to communicate with our spouses. Communication is essentially our ability to send or receive messages from each other. In marital relationships, not only are we transmitting messages to our spouses, but we also share our feelings, thoughts, and closeness as we communicate. The tone of voice and body language also convey thoughts and feelings. You would be amazed at the number of marriages that have failed because of lack of communication or poor communication. Communication is not only sending and receiving messages, another key part of communication is the way we listen and digest the messages that we are receiving.

TYPES OF LISTENING

Active or attentive listening

As the name implies, attentive listening is listening attentively. This includes what is being said and the method in which it is being conveyed to you. Attentive listening may sound easy, but it is one of the most difficult types of listening. This is because it requires your complete and undivided attention. Think how many times we are distracted during the normal course of our daily events. Even in listening, we get distracted.

Passive listening

In passive listening, the listening spouse is basically listening with one ear, so to speak. In other words, he or she is hearing, but not actually listening. In passive listening, the listening spouse is less interested in the topic of discussion, probably because he or she is the guilty party, or is fed up, or just doesn't care. Consider a couple who is discussing some issues affecting their marriage. The wife notices that her husband is not really paying attention or is listening passively. The wife asks if he can pay attention to what she is saying to enable them to attempt to resolve their issues. His response: "Honey, save that for someone who cares." With that type of disrespect or listening, a marriage in that mode is more apt to fall apart.

Selective listening

In this type of listening, you select exactly what you want to hear and make a conscious effort to exclude what you do not want to hear. There may be some painful issues in the marriage that the listener is avoiding and does not want to recall. Sometimes there is no rhyme or reason as to why the listener chooses to be selective. One thing is clear, however: the listener is uninterested in the subject of the discussion. Can you imagine what this type of listening will do to a marriage?

Avoid doubts in listening patterns

Communication is one of the key elements needed for a marriage to keep growing and blossoming. The way that we listen or process the message that we received is also a critical factor of that communication process. To avoid doubts in listening patterns, consider the following:

The "I" clarification is personalizing your listening pattern to focus on your spouse: "I understand you, darling." If your spouse feels and perceives those personalization, both the spouse giving and receiving the message are on the same page. Interaction becomes meaningful and understanding enhanced. The "I" statement leaves no ambiguity. Imagine this response at the end of a statement from the spouse who is listening: "I know exactly what you mean, honey." How much clearer could that be? The "I" statements or responses shows our spouses how attentive our listening is at the time of receiving the message. It further shows our sensitivity to our spouses and shows how much we value our marriage.

Prioritization

We should always make our spouses a priority in our dealings. You may ask what that has to do with answering doubts in listening patterns. The answer is that sometimes we tend to take our spouses for granted. We tend to make time for everything and for everybody, with the exception of our spouses. We make time for appointments we have in the office. When we are at home and

LOVE AND MARRIAGE PERSPECTIVES

a colleague calls about a problem he or she is having, we leave everything and run to help. When an out-of-town business associate is in town and calls, we leave our spouses and run to the hotel where the business associate is staying. We come home and there is a meeting at our golf club -- you guessed it, we drop everything and go. Sometimes when we are out of town on a business trip, we fail even to call our spouses and check on them. We may not listen to the body language of our spouses about the neglect by not giving them time, but we seem to have time for other people. If we make our spouses our priority, we are sending a clear message that we care, for our actions also communicate that care. We can take our spouses to some of those appointments. We can also take them out of town, or we can even cancel some of those appointments and give our spouses that time.

In conclusion, remember that regardless of your listening skills and how well you practice them, miscommunications are still bound to occur. It is up to the individuals in that marriage to find appropriate mechanisms for what works for them. The key thing to bear in mind is that there is no panacea for effective communication or active listening. The trend, direction, and effectiveness of communication in marriage rest squarely and solely on the couple involved.

The single biggest problem in communication is the illusion that it has taken place.
—George Bernard Shaw

CHAPTER SEVEN

Sexual Attitudes, Patterns, And Exclusivity In Marriage

Obviously, in dealing with a relationship, sexuality has to be involved, and jealousy and emotions like that. And I don't know, I've always been intrigued by those emotions.
—Adrian Lyne

SEX IS A difficult subject to discuss. This is because opinions on sexual perceptions, beliefs, and attitudes are many and varied. In discussing issues of this nature, you want to be as accommodating as possible without losing or sacrificing the content and logic of your presentation. When some people venture to discuss sex, it is with much caution and uneasiness. Nevertheless, a book on marriage, even Christian marriage, is not deemed complete without mention of sexuality in the context of a marriage, albeit briefly.

Disclaimer

It is appropriate to state that the intention of this chapter is to discuss a sexual relationship in the context of marriage. It is not the intention of this chapter to judge or legislate certain sexual conduct or tell married couples what to do in their marital lives. Certain issues discussed are supposed to be for the benefit or betterment of marriage. The choice however, rests solely on couples since they are the ultimate arbiters in their marriages.

Where it all started

In the beginning, God created Adam. God noticed that Adam was incomplete because he was alone, and God never wanted man to be alone. God thought of what to do about Adam's isolation. After thoughtful scenarios, an idea came to him. As an apparent solution to Adam's incompleteness, he created a woman named Eve, as a wife and a gift to Adam, allowing them to be together and enjoy God's love while experiencing the love of each other. God's plan called for marital harmony through the unification of Adam and Eve as a conduit for spiritual wholeness. As Adam and Eve shared that human love, they became appreciative of spiritual love with God, but something went terribly wrong in the Garden of Eden, as we all know. It is believed that whatever went wrong has continued to hurt mankind, as the repercussions have been profound in our history. God wasted no time in making his displeasure known to Adam and Eve as well as the serpent. His pronouncements were direct, severe, and profound. To the serpent, God said:

> *Because you have done this, you are cursed more than all cattle, and more than every beast of the field; on your belly*

SEXUAL ATTITUDES, PATTERNS, AND EXCLUSIVITY IN MARRIAGE

you shall go, and you shall eat dust all the days of your life. And I will put enmity between you and the woman, and between your seed and her seed; he shall bruise your head, and you shall bruise his heel. (Genesis 3:14–15)

He said to Eve:

I will greatly multiply your sorrow and your conception; in pain you shall bring forth children; your desire shall be for your husband, and he shall rule over you. (Genesis 3:16)

And to Adam:

Cursed is the ground for your sake; in toil you shall eat of it all the days of your life. Both thorns and thistles it shall bring forth for you, and you shall eat the herb of the field. In the sweat of your face you shall eat bread till you return to the ground, for out of it you were taken; for dust you are, and to dust you shall return. (Genesis 3:17–19)

Looking at all these pronouncements, we can see that they continue to be true, having profound effect on men and women today, even as we read this book.

Sexual attitude and perceptions in marriage

People's attitudes, perceptions, and understanding of sexual issues are varied and diversified. That diversity stems from our different personalities and our families' beliefs and attitudes about sex. Family is one of the agencies of socialization. Sexual values and perceptions are first absorbed through family of origin and later further influenced by friends. In some families, there is no discussion of sex whatsoever.

Sex for the wrong reasons

Sex in marriage is a gift from God. Marital sexual intercourse should not be seen as a perfect performance, for nothing is perfect. Marital intercourse is a mutual commitment wherein married couples should enjoy intimacy, sharing it between a husband and a wife. Even in marriage, when sex is given for the wrong reasons, it has its consequences and ramifications. Sex in marriage requires honesty and mutual commitment for the gift of sex to be meaningful. If honesty is lacking, intimacy is absent when sex is given for the wrong reasons. Deep and innermost sharing that characterizes marital intimacy is also absent. You do not have to be a rocket scientist to know that sex with your marital mate does not require great expertise but a deep caring, appreciation, and acceptance of each other.

If your spouse is angry at you and you give him/her sex as an appeasement, that falls within the context of sex given for the wrong reasons. That sex is then conditional and is not mutual sharing within the context of the give-and-take required in marriage, in that it lacks mutuality. Giving sex to get the love of your partner is not only unhealthy, but also falls within the purview of sex given for the wrong reasons. The giver feels that the more he or she has sex with the spouse, the more that spouse should love him or her. It does not necessarily happen that way. You should have already been in love before marriage. Sex to get love also traps the individual, for if you do not give sex for whatever reason, does it mean that the love will evaporate?

What about giving sex to prevent your partner from seeing someone else? This is also unhealthy sex, falling within the ambit of sex given for the wrong reason. The danger here is that your partner may be seeing someone already. Were you not giving him or her sex prior to that infidelity? There is also a possibility that he or she may continue to see that person even after you continue having sex. Marriage counseling appears appropriate in that instance because there are some mental health issues present in that situation. Sex is a precious commodity, and if misused or abused, it can lead to vulnerability and sexual addiction. That is how damaging sex used or given for the wrong reasons can be. Let us now review use or misuse of sex.

Use and misuse of sex

When sex is separated from true love, the resultant effect is misuse. Sexual intercourse outside the limits of marriage is viewed as inappropriate. The scripture frowns against it. Because it is misuse of sex, it hurts the feelings of your spouse. Sex in marriage is characterized by affection, trust, and caring for each other. When sex in marriage lacks those characteristics and mutuality, deep sharing of thoughts, feelings, affections, and emotions, sex then becomes worthless. The couple at this point is just having sex for the sake of having sex. Intimacy is absent, as are all other attendant factors that convey the true meaning of sex in marriage.

When a spouse manipulates the other spouse into having sex for his or her own selfish purposes, it is a misuse of sex. God created us because He loved us. With that love in mind, he instituted marriage to unite a man and a woman in holy matrimony as a precursor to sex for the natural and exclusive enjoyment of husbands and wives. Sex in marriage is incumbent on commitment and puritanical love that has deep Biblical and spiritual roots. That is why excursions outside of marriage, which are universally seen as disdainful, should be avoided. Couples talk about sexual fulfillment in marriage, and for couples that approach sex with some ulterior motive, that fulfillment will continue to remain an illusion. So long as love is separated from sex, that sexual fulfillment will remain elusive—and at best, a sheer fantasy unfulfilled.

Sexual exclusivity in marriage

Some define marriage as a commitment between a husband and a wife. Legally it is a binding contract between spouses. Christian marriage is a combination of the above but is also a covenant as made to humanity by God and revealed through the scripture. Looking at the above three definitions of marriages, there appears to be no doubt that a spouse can be angry or distraught if

SEXUAL ATTITUDES, PATTERNS, AND EXCLUSIVITY IN MARRIAGE

that commitment, contract, or covenant is violated or breached. This is so in that the commitment, contract, or covenant is between two spouses. There was no third party in this arrangement, which signifies exclusivity -- hence "three is a crowd," and any other persons intruding in the marriage are violating that exclusiveness.

There is no doubt that sex creates intense bonding between couples in a marriage. With that bonding comes intense commitment. As this intense commitment becomes stronger, possessiveness progresses to the next stage. This possessiveness becomes a precursor to healthy jealousy, which then translates to exclusivity. The exclusiveness in marital sex is a way for the couple to affirm their commitment, uniqueness, and specialness to each other. Exclusivity is also an extension of the marital vow, wherein both spouses pledge their love for each other regardless of the circumstances.

Everybody has a personal relationship with God. He relates individually to each person and wants a personal commitment. Marital love mimics personal commitment the same way we commit our lives to God. It then follows that as couples reserve themselves for each other, they are demonstrating their understanding of God's love and exclusivity for one another. Physical love and spiritual love are not mutually exclusive, for one complements the other. Marital exclusively falls back to God's original intention, plan, and design for marriage, which is sharing your love exclusively with your spouse.

Lack of exclusivity degrades sexual dignity. Deep sharing and commitment are lacking as sex becomes a matter of performance, which is superficial, as opposed to sharing and commitment, which are deep and innermost. We as humans are made in the image of God, and therefore we should operate as God wants us to. That means following God's plan regarding sex, which is between a woman and a man in the context of a marriage relationship.

Sex as a gift of marriage

Somewhere in this book, I stated that passion is the gift of marriage; sex is the ultimate, exclusive, and unique gift of marriage. Let us discuss these three gifts.

Ultimate gift

In this instance, "ultimate" means that sex is the extreme way of expressing your affection, love, and feelings toward your partner. It is the most absolute and supreme expression, for with sex, you have given him/her your innermost self. This is part of the reason most couples are advised to wait for sex until marriage, for once you have given yourself, what is given cannot be taken back.

SEXUAL ATTITUDES, PATTERNS, AND EXCLUSIVITY IN MARRIAGE

An exclusive gift

It is an exclusive gift, for sex is designed exclusively for two people in a marriage situation. It is exclusively for two people married to each other to enjoy. In this situation, sex is reserved solely, undividedly, and exclusively, and it therefore becomes the exclusive right of those two individuals. Any person trying to intrude is going against the covenant of God and marriage.

A unique gift

Sex is a unique feeling that two individuals in marriage experience. The feeling the couple derives from sex is a unique feeling that only two of them can relate to. It is their right to have and enjoy that one-of-a kind feeling that God reserved for only the two of them in their union.

God's intention for sex in marriage

The most poignant question for most people is, does God truly intend for sex to be experienced within the context of marriage? I will respond with one word to make my answer absolutely and unequivocally clear: *yes*. God truly intended for sex to be experienced in marriage. The scripture stated:

God richly gave us all things to enjoy. (I Timothy 6:17)

LOVE AND MARRIAGE PERSPECTIVES

So yes, that includes sex, but in the context of a marital relationship. The book of Solomon, also called the Song of Solomon, is the most romantic expression of sexuality in the Bible. There is sometimes a tendency for some people to read things, including the Bible, in a hurry, without actually understanding the true meaning of what they read. But the more people read the Bible, the more they discover and understand the true meaning of what they are reading. An initial reader of the Song of Solomon will pause to wonder whether he or she is actually reading from the Bible. The Song of Solomon starts with:

Let him kiss me with the kisses of his mouth: for your love is better than wine. (Song of Solomon 1:2)

The Song of Solomon has eight chapters. It used the words love and lovely sixty-two times to address and express their love for each other. This love is between Solomon and the Shulamite woman. Here are spouses expressing their passionate love and to show that they are spouses, the Song of Solomon also used the word spouse nine times. Merriam-Webster defines spouse as one's husband or wife. Their writings to each other had meaning since they were husband and wife, especially in chapter seven, with writings that would floor a woman with affection in greeting cards of today. Here are a few verses of that chapter:

How beautiful are your feet in sandals, O prince's daughter! The curves of your thighs are like jewels, the work of the hands of a skillful workman. Your navel is a rounded

SEXUAL ATTITUDES, PATTERNS, AND EXCLUSIVITY IN MARRIAGE

goblet; it lacks no blended beverage. Your waist is a heap of wheat set about with lilies. Your two breasts are like two fawns, twins of a gazelle. (Song of Solomon 7:1–3)

The point intended here is that the Song of Solomon painted a perfect picture of marital love, wherein spouses should enjoy sex in the context of a marital relationship. It shows how lovely, uniquely, passionately, ultimately, exclusively, and intimately spouses should be as they enjoy each other in those things or areas exclusively reserved for two people in a marriage. God's intention is for a husband and wife to enjoy each other completely within the covenant of a marriage. Marital intercourse is condoned and encouraged in the Bible, whereby husband and wife become one flesh and one body.

For this reason a man shall leave his father and mother and be joined to his wife, and the two shall become one flesh. (Ephesians 5:31)

When man and woman become husband and wife, the responsibility of caring for and pleasing each other follows. The Bible states:

But he who is married cares about the things of the world— how he may please his wife. (I Corinthians 7:33)

The most poignant is when couples were advised not to refuse each other. The Bible further states as follows:

> *Nevertheless, because of sexual immorality, let each man have his own wife, and each woman have her own husband. Let the husband render to his wife the affection due her, and likewise also the wife to her husband. The wife does not have authority over her body, but the husband does. And likewise the husband does not have authority over his own body, but the wife does. Do not deprive each another except with the consent for a time that you may give yourselves to fasting and prayer; and come together again so that Satan does not tempt you because of your lack of self-control.* (1 Corinthians 7:2-5)

Anderson and Anderson (2003, 148–49) stated: "The truth is that sex is God-given. It is intended for marriage. It is meant for procreation, but it is also meant for fun. Sexual intimacy is the greatest high that our bodies were designed for. Without regular sex and good sex in marriage, temptation may come your way. Biblical sex means all sexual activity between husband and wife that they agree to is uncontrolled by boundaries that hinder mutual pleasure."

Some points to consider

(1) "Let your fountain be blessed, and rejoice with the wife of your youth. As a loving deer and a graceful doe, let her breasts satisfy you at all times; and always be enraptured with her love." (Proverbs 5:18–19)

SEXUAL ATTITUDES, PATTERNS, AND EXCLUSIVITY IN MARRIAGE

(2) "Do not deprive one another except with consent for a time, that you may give yourselves to fasting and prayer; and come together again so that Satan does not tempt you because of your lack of self-control." (I Corinthians 7:5)

(3) "The wife does not have authority over her own body, but the husband does. And likewise the husband does not have authority over his own body but the wife does." (I Corinthians 7:4)

(4) "But I say to the unmarried and to the widows: it is good for them if they remain even as I am." (I Corinthians 7:8)

(5) "Nevertheless, because of sexual immorality, let each man have his own wife, and let each woman have her own husband." (I Corinthians 7:2)

(6) "Let the husband render to his wife the affection due her, and likewise also the wife to her husband." (I Corinthians 7:3)

(7) "But he who is married cares about the things of the world—how he may please his wife." (I Corinthians 7:33)

(8) "There is a difference between a wife and a virgin. The unmarried woman cares about the things of the Lord, that she may be holy both in body and in spirit. But she who is married cares about the things of the world—how she may please her husband. And this I say for your own profit, not that I may put a leash on you, but for what is proper, and that you may serve the

LOVE AND MARRIAGE PERSPECTIVES

Lord without distraction." (I Corinthians 7:34–35)

There are more citations or quotations from the scripture. It seems appropriate to stop at the juncture, however, because the point of Biblical discussions of sex has been made.

I'd thought sexuality was instinctive or natural, but it's profoundly linked to inner security and cultural context.
—Tahar Ben Jelloun

CHAPTER EIGHT
Resolving Marital Conflicts

Conflict builds character. Crisis defines it.
—Steven V. Thuton

BARTOS AND WEHR (2002) defined conflict in this way: "A situation in which actors use conflict action against each other to attain incompatible goals and/or to express their hostility."

Hardly any marriages have never experienced conflict. Conflict is a functional part of marriage and a testing of the foundation of marriage. The frequency of the conflict and the degree of the successful resolution or failure of the resolution most of the time dictates the direction in which the marriage is going. A well-grounded marriage has fewer marital conflicts than a shaky, vulnerable marriage. The issue is not whether a conflict will occur, but when. When it does happen, that is when and where the couple's conflict resolution skills come into play. The marriage of the couple with good conflict resolution skills is more likely to survive as opposed to the couple that lacks conflict resolution skills. A conflict not managed appropriately can destroy a marriage. It is necessary for couples to learn ways of managing and resolving conflict. When there is a conflict in a relationship and it is mismanaged, the relationship becomes cold and distant.

Some techniques of resolution

Some techniques or approaches to resolving conflict in marriage include the don't-ask-me-and-I-won't-tell-you approach, the limping approach, the conference approach, the in-your-face approach, the makeup approach, and the "whatever" approach. It appears pertinent to review each approach at this time and explore how it impacts marital conflict and resolution.

The don't-ask-me-and-I-won't-tell-you approach

In this technique, the couple is afraid to discuss the issue. They know that there is a problem, but they decide to leave it alone as if nothing happened. The inherent danger with this approach is that the problem will not go away. The problem will be ticking like a time bomb until it finally explodes, leading to the demise of the marriage.

The limping approach

In this scenario, the couple makes a superficial attempt to talk about the problem, but with no resolution. The marriage limps along, hence the limping approach. When a marriage is at a "limping along" stage, it shows that the marriage is not completely healthy.

The conference approach

This approach is where the couple sits down in an orderly fashion like two people at a business conference, marshaling out their points and discussing issues seriously and respectfully. The objective of the conference is to have a heartfelt dialogue with the intention of reaching a resolution that is conducive to both parties and also serves the best interest of the relationship. Couples who use this approach have the greatest chance of resolving their conflicts, and their relationship lasts longer and becomes more meaningful.

In-your-face approach

The couple is disorderly in this approach. One or both people point accusing fingers at each other. They talk out of turn. They are loud, and respect is out the window. There may be cursing as they talk to one another. Undoubtedly, nothing is resolved with this approach. In some instances, the couple ends up worse than they were before they started, in that feelings are now hurt because of the commotion and insults traded in the name of resolving conflict.

The makeup approach

In this approach, the couple uses sex to make up any differences they have in their marital situation. Whenever any conflict arises, the other offending party will talk about how he or she will make it up to the other spouse. The danger with this approach is that the couple becomes more interested in satisfying their urges or sexual feelings by using sex as a way of resolving conflict.

The "whatever" approach

With this technique or situation, one of the spouses adopts the response "whatever" to any situations or issue discussed. This can be for two reasons. First, he or she is toeing the line of the marriage and does not want to be seen as the one who torpedoed the marriage. Second, one of the spouses can be so fed up with the marriage that he or she does not care anymore, in which case any decision or resolution will suffice. Essentially, with this scenario, the marriage is already dead. What is left for the marriage is to make the funeral arrangements.

What is the best way to handle conflict in a marriage?

Let bygones be bygones

When a conflict is already resolved, move on; do not bring it up later, during the process of resolving another conflict. Bringing back previous resolved issues flares up emotions of that issue, thereby bringing that issue back from the dead. Just as if you have already forgiven someone, let the issue go. An example will make this more illustrative.

RESOLVING MARITAL CONFLICTS

Kevin and Kendra have marital conflicts, just like any other couple. Kendra has a habit of escalating issues when she and Kevin attempt to resolve their conflicts. In one of their stormy sessions, despite Kendra's being the guilty party, she told Kevin that she was not going to apologize for her misdeeds. She also rescinded all the apologies she had given in previous sessions they'd had. That last straw ended any meaningful resolution to their marital discord. Their marriage terminated because of that statement. Two lessons are clear in this scenario. First, in marital resolutions, think through what you want to say and say it respectfully. In other words, approach the resolution with forethought and do not express your feelings impulsively. Second, since the objective of such meetings is to progress the marriage and not regress it, we should always strive for a timely and meaningful resolution for the sake of the marriage.

In this scenario, Kendra, instead of attempting to compromise, let her impulsivity get in the way of a meaningful compromise. The marriage not only suffered as result of that, but it ended abruptly. In marriage, when you compromise and surrender, it does not mean that you are weak. As a smart general, you have instead saved your marriage for another day.

Let us explore the case of Lyndon and Lanett. This couple always approached issues from the view that they are humans, and there are therefore bound to be mistakes and conflicts. Both spouses take responsibility for their actions or behaviors during the conflict resolution sessions. They always reach a compromise, and

Lanett put it succinctly when she confided to her friend that she and Lyndon are one flesh, by virtue of their marriage—and that when she reaches a compromise with Lyndon, that compromise is with herself. Likewise, when she surrenders to Lyndon, she is also surrendering to herself. This couple just celebrated their twenty-second anniversary. Compromise and surrender techniques appear to be a great tool to their marital resolution. Their personalities are probably similar.

Win-win situation

In resolving marital issues, the objective is not who won or who lost. Remember that in marriage, both of you are one, and being one, it follows that if one spouse loses, both spouses do. The rationale behind the win-win approach is that not only did both of you win by resolving the issues at hand, but that the marriage also won by being safe, meaningful, and productive. Spouses should sit down as equal partners and try to resolve differences amicably, bearing the best interests of the marriage in mind. With this approach, there is no victor, no vanquished -- just winners, hence the win-win approach.

Active listening

You would be amazed how little couples who want to get their viewpoints across listen to each other. Active listening is a major key or ingredient in marital resolution. The more you listen to your spouse, the more you tend to understand his or her grievance. The more he or she states her grievance, the more likelihood there is for that spouse to listen actively when you state your own grievance, thereby giving both spouses an attempt at trying to resolve the issue.

Be respectful

Avoid harmful words. Ephesians 4:29 states:

> *Let no corrupt word proceed out of your mouth, but what is good for necessary edification, that it may impart grace to the hearers.*

If you approach conflict resolution from the point of respect toward your spouse, not only will you have smoother sailing, but you also get respect in return. Your partner will work with you more meaningfully if he or she perceives respect in the course of the discussion or resolution. It follows that there should not be name-calling or disparaging, deprecating remarks, and with that type of environment, both spouses may even appreciate each other more, thereby giving the relationship an added boost or punch.

Reciprocate feelings

One of the objectives of conflict resolution is to resolve a presenting conflict and enhance a healthy marriage. It is always a good practice to start the resolution process with a prayer toward the issue and then follow it with a hug; then the couple can start discussing the issue at hand. What the couple accomplishes is bringing God into the midst of their discussion. The second accomplishment is that with a hug, you feel love and re-express your commitment toward each other through nonverbal communication. Chances of resolving a conflict are better in that type of cordial environment.

Reward system

It is pertinent to give each other a pat on the back when a conflict is successfully resolved. The couple can even take it a step further by going out for dinner or a night out at one of their favorite places. When an issue is not resolved, do not throw your hands up in the air and give up. Make a commitment to each other to attempt to resolve that issue at another time. Leaving a problem unresolved or acting as if it does not exist is a recipe for disaster and may ultimately become the beginning of the demise for a marriage.

Compromise/surrender technique

A smart general is he who lives another day to fight his battle. In marriage, the objective is to avoid any fighting and keep the marriage alive. The cardinal principle of this technique is to resolve conflicts through verbal means and compromise. In the course of the resolution, one spouse has to surrender to the other, regardless of who is the guilty party, for the compromise to hold. A peaceful marriage is an accomplished marriage. Romans 14:19 succinctly noted:

> *Therefore let us pursue the things which make for peace and the things by which one may edify another.*

The greatest conflicts are not between two people but between one person and himself.
—Garth Brooks

CHAPTER NINE
Prayer And Marriage

It is better in prayer to have a heart without words than words without a heart.

—Mahatma Gandhi

PRAYER IS A communication between the person praying and his or her God. It is also a medium in which the person praying presents petitions, requests, and supplications to God and expects a favorable answer. Put another way, as we pray, we expect our wishes or supplications to be granted. Some see prayer as a conversation with God or meditation to God. Either way you look at it, we align ourselves to our creator as we lift up our souls to pray, believing that our petition will be granted. The Psalm of David illustrates this:

> *To you, O Lord, I lift up my soul. O my God, I trust in You; let me not be ashamed; let not my enemies triumph over me.* (Psalm 25:1–2)

What do we expect?

As couples, we expect to receive what we ask for. God wants us to ask for what we want. In John 14:14, He stated:

LOVE AND MARRIAGE PERSPECTIVES

If you ask anything in My name, I will do it.

And in Matthew 7:7–8:

Ask, and it will be given to you; seek, and you will find; knock, and it will be opened to you. For everyone who asks receives, and he who seeks finds, and to him who knocks it will be opened.

The condition isn't only to ask, but the key phrase is to ask in God's name. We have to understand, however, that having our prayers answered is not automatic and involves waiting:

Rest in the Lord, and wait patiently for Him; do not fret because of Him who prospers in his way. (Psalm 37:7)

We cannot rush God. He knows the right time to grant our request. Our actions in marriage count as we wait for our petitions to be granted. If we go back and start cursing our spouses or contravening our marriage vows while waiting for our petition to be granted, do you think that God will grant our request? I do not think that he would. That is why we should not do things that are detrimental to our marriages and to other people. Our actions reflect who we are, both in marriage and in our dealings with others. Whether or not we are waiting for supplications to be granted, we should always strive to be filled with the Holy Spirit, and the way to achieve that is to avoid sin. Take into account that God can come again at any time, and we will be required to account for our stewardship. Don't you want to be ready for that day? I think that it is best to be ready rather than be caught unawares or unprepared.

Are our petitions answered all the time?

Our petitions or requests may not be answered all the time, probably because of our actions after our supplication to God during the waiting period. This is a good reason to always be on our best behavior in marriage. The way we ask or what we ask God to do for us may be the problem. Let us review those two issues.

What we ask for

In Matthew 6:33, He stated:

> *But seek first the kingdom of God and His righteousness, and all these things shall be added to you.*

This shows that sometimes we pray for the wrong reasons and ask for the wrong things. Remember what happened when the Lord appeared to Solomon in a dream and said:

> *"Ask! What shall I give you?"* (I Kings 3:5)

Solomon never asked for riches, just the ability to discern justice among his people. He pleased God by asking for that. God gave him what he asked for and added other things that he did not ask for:

> *Then God said to him: "Because you have asked this thing, and have not asked long life for yourself, not have asked for riches for yourself, nor have asked the life of your enemies, but have asked for yourself understanding to discern justice, behold, I have done according to your words; see, I have given you a wise and understanding heart, so that there has not been anyone like you before you, nor shall any like you arise after you. And I have also given you what you have not asked: both riches and honor, so that there shall not be anyone like you among the kings all your days. So if you walk in My ways, to keep My statutes and My commandments, as your father David walked, then I will lengthen your days."* (I Kings 3:11–14)

That is an example of knowing what to ask for. Can you imagine if God approached me prior to the days when I understood the scriptures as I do now and asked me to state what I want, saying that he would give it to me? Instead of Solomon's approach, my approach would erroneously have been to clear my voice without humbling myself and arrogantly ask as follows: "Lord, I am having problems with my mortgage. I want you to make my mortgage payments." I would then be trying to command God. I probably wouldn't even have used the words appreciate or help to state my request. This would be better: "Lord, I would appreciate your help in making my mortgage payments." Back to my request: "Lord, can I get a new car and a new house? I want to be the first one to live in a house, and I also like that new car smell. I am tired of being poor. Can I have all the money that I will spend the rest of my life and that of my children? I do not want to go to work again, because I do not get along with my supervisor at work." I would also have a list of other things that I wanted to ask God for. From the way that I presented my petition and the tone of my request above, do you think that God would grant my request? He probably wouldn't. So in prayers, we are being renewed day by day and counseled not to lose hope and heart as follows:

> *Therefore we do not lose heart. Even though our outward man is perishing, yet the inward man is being renewed day by day. For our light affliction, which is but for a moment, is working for us a far more exceeding and eternal weight of glory, while we do not look at the things which are seen, but the things that are not seen. For the things which are seen are temporary, but the things which are not seen are eternal.* (2 Corinthians 4:16–18)

The way we ask

Prayer in marriage is very important. The way you pray and ask for your petitions is up to you and God. The most important thing is that you and your spouse are praying.

> *Pray without ceasing.* (I Thessalonians 5:17)

LOVE AND MARRIAGE PERSPECTIVES

As you pray in marriage, you put your marriage in his hands and take him as your refuge, rock, and fortress.

> *The Lord is my rock and my fortress and my deliverer; My God, my strength, in whom I will trust; my shield and the horn of my salvation, my stronghold.* (Psalm 18:2)

Again, the way we present our prayer matters in the eyes of the Lord, both what is in our hearts and what comes out of our mouth.

> *Let the words of my mouth and the mediation of my heart be acceptable in Your sight, O Lord, my strength and my redeemer.* (Psalm 19:14)

To illustrate the way we should pray, let us review the case of the Pharisee and the tax collector. Our humility and what comes out of our mouths, hearts, and souls matters. Take into account that our mouths speak out what is in our hearts. Remember how the Pharisee was bragging about his fasting, how upright he was, and how he did not extort people like the tax collector praying on the other side? The tax collector, on the other hand, was humbly asking God for his compassionate mercy. This is what Jesus said about that parable in regard to the man that was arrogant and the one that was humble.

> *I tell you, this man went down to his house justified rather than the other; for everyone who exalts himself will*

be humbled, and he who humbles himself will be exalted. (Luke 18:14)

It shows that the way you pray or the way you present supplication is everything. In proverbs, It is further stated that:

Before honor is humility. (Proverbs 15:33)

Those who seek me diligently will find me. (Proverbs 8:17)

So if we continue to diligently seek him and pray humbly, he may grant our petition. However, this is contingent on our relationship with him, what we are asking for, and whether he perceives that what we are asking for is in our best interest—and in the best interest of our spouses. It also depends on how patiently we want to wait for our prayers to be answered.

I waited patiently for the Lord, and he inclined to me and heard my cry. He also brought me up out of a horrible pit, out of the miry clay, and set my feet up on a rock, and established my steps. (Psalm 40:1–2)

Praise and thanksgiving to God

God may sometimes grant our request. In the euphoria of our request being granted by him, we forget to feel obligated to thank him or praise him for what he has done for us. If we cannot even thank God for what he did for us, what makes us think that he will be willing to do something for us next time around? As we humble ourselves, we praise and exalt him.

> *I will bless the Lord at all times; His praise shall continually be in my mouth. My soul shall make its boast in the Lord; the humble shall hear of it and be glad. Oh, magnify the Lord with me, and let us exalt His name together.* (Psalm 34:1–3)

That reminds me of a time when a good friend of mine was asking me what was the best way to praise God. My response was that we are all grown, and we all know what is good, humble, and noble in the eyes of the Lord. That we know what is good to say about the Lord. That he, my friend, should go and do likewise. Finally, I referred him to the scripture quoted below:

> *Finally brethren, whatever things are true, whatever things are noble, whatever things are just, whatever things are pure, whatever things are lovely, whatever things are of good report, if there is any virtue and if there is anything praiseworthy—meditate on these things.* (Philippians 4:8)

Further, remember that as we give thanks and praise to God, we also have peace in ourselves and with our spouses. The peace we have in ourselves also translates to peace with God. This peace with God enhances our relationship with him, thereby opening us up for him to grant our petition.

Be anxious for nothing, but in everything by prayer and supplication, with thanksgiving, let your requests be made known to God; and the peace of God, which surpasses all understanding, will guard your hearts and minds through Christ Jesus. (Philippians 4:6–7)

Praising the Lord has added benefits. I am assuming that you are married and probably have at least one child. How do you feel when your child asks for money to buy ice cream when the ice cream truck is on the street and other kids are buying ice cream? Let us assume that you give your child the money, and after buying the ice cream, he or she comes to you and thanks and praises you profusely for your kind gesture. Based on his or her politeness and appreciation, if that child asks for another favor, there is a high probability that you will give again the next time. That is the added benefit of appreciating and praising.

Praise the Lord, O my soul, and forget not all His benefits. (Psalm 103:2)

Praising and thanking God for all the favors past received and favors yet to receive sets us up for a better relationship with God. As we give thanks, we recognize and affirm the authority of God.

You are my God, and I will praise You; You are my God, and I will praise you; You are my god, I will exalt You. Oh, give thanks to the Lord, for He is good! For His mercy endures forever. (Psalm 118:28–29)

LOVE AND MARRIAGE PERSPECTIVES

Thanksgiving and praise to God is not only for answering our petitions and requests. It is also for everyday life. It is for all the things that happened to us. God is in control of our lives. He is also in control of our marriage, children, our jobs, and all of our undertakings. He is in charge of all things, and when I say all things, I mean all things.

> *In everything give thanks; for this is the will of God in Christ Jesus for you.* (I Thessalonians 5:18)

There is no specific time for praising. It is up to you and your spouse to know when the time is conductive for praising. Regardless of when you give praise, the key thing is to make sure that it is from your heart.

> *I will praise the Lord, who counsels me; even at night my heart instructs me. I have set the Lord always before me. Because he is at my right hand I will not be shaken.* (Psalm 16:7–8) NIV

Interrelatedness between prayer and marriage

A critical thinker might observe some interrelatedness between prayer and marriage. By this, I mean certain things that we achieve from praying—things that also enhance our marriage. These things include communication, commitment, passion, intimacy, understanding, faithfulness, and bonding. Let us review each of these things, and how they are achieved through praying—specifically, how they enhance and impact marriages.

Communication

Praying is a way of communicating with God. As we pray, we are talking to God, transmitting and communicating our feelings, hopes, aspirations, emotions, desires, problems, and woes. In marriage, communication is a key ingredient in enhancing marriage. Technically, if there is no communication, there is no meaningful marriage. When you do not communicate with your spouse, your marriage is stagnant and unenhanced. As you pray to God and communicate with him, your life is meaningful and enhanced. Can you imagine how unfulfilled our lives would be if we did not know God, never prayed, and never had dialogue with our creator? Is it not like driving a car at one hundred miles per hour on a freeway with our eyes closed? Praying keeps us in touch with God, and without praying, our lives are nothing. Who wants a meaningless, nothingness life or an unfulfilled, meaningless marriage? The interrelatedness is those feelings, emotions, aspirations, dreams, desires, problems, and woes as we communicate to God; we communicate the same thing to our spouses. The more open we are in communicating our feelings to God, the more he understands us. In marriage, the more open we are with our spouses about those feelings, the more our spouses understand us, thereby enhancing our marriage. It makes more sense and imperative to pray together with our spouses to not only achieve those objectives with God, but also in our marriages.

LOVE AND MARRIAGE PERSPECTIVES

Commitment

Random House Webster's Dictionary defines commitment in this way: "to give in trust or charge; to bind or obligate as by pledge; and to perform or perpetrate."

Let us look at that definition and see how it relates to prayer and marriage. Consider the word "give." As we pray, we give our lives to God. We also give our marriages to God. The next important word is "trust." Every Christian trusts in God, and by praying, we show trust in him, just as we trust our spouses. Are you going to pray to something that you do not trust?

When we lift our souls to the Lord, it means that we give our lives, hearts, and souls to the Lord.

> *To you, O Lord, I lift up my soul. O God, I trust you.* (Psalm 25:1–2)

> *Keep my soul, and deliver me. Let me not be ashamed, for I put my trust in you.* (Psalm 25:20)

Trusting in the Lord is not a wasted trust. In fact, it is an absolute trust. When you trust in the Lord, he will not fail you. He will be a pillar of support and a house of refuge for you.

> *He who dwells in the secret place of the Most High shall abide under the shadow of the Almighty. I will say of the*

Lord, He is my refuge and my fortress; My God, in Him I will trust. (Psalm 91:1–2)

Back to our dictionary definition of commitment, the next key word is "charge," meaning to take charge. As we pray, we let God take charge or control of our lives, including things like our jobs, our relationships with our spouses and families, and every aspect of our dealings with others. When God is in charge or takes control, we have no fear and we are empowered. The only fear is the fear of the Lord.

The Lord is my light and my salvation, whom shall I fear? The Lord is the strength of my life; of whom shall I be afraid? (Psalm 27:1)

Another key word in that definition is "bind." Prayer ensures bonding with God. As we pray continually or pray without ceasing, we feel closer to God. There is definitely a correlation between praying and bonding with God. In other words, the more we pray, the more we bond with God. The more we bond with God, the more we are in a position that our supplication will be granted. That granting of our request comes with commitment with God through prayers.

Commit to the Lord whatever you do and your plans will succeed. (Proverbs 16:3) NIV

LOVE AND MARRIAGE PERSPECTIVES

In relating commitment and bonding to marriage, we like to be, want to be, and should be committed to our spouses. We should not let world distractions, detractions, and temptations shake our commitment or resolve to our spouses. The same way that we bond to God through our prayers is the same way we should bond with our spouses.

The word "obligate" shows our obligation as Christians to maintain a relationship with God. We are also obligated to love our spouses. We are obligated to keep the commandments of God. This obligates us to be faithful to God by not having other gods. Similarly, we are obligated to be faithful to our spouses by not having affairs behind their backs.

Now to the three *Ps*: "pledge, perform, and perpetrate." I will explain them in that order. We pledge our love allegiance to God. With that pledge comes an obligation of things that we must do, such as praying. With that pledge comes the commitment to do what we pledged. It is the same scenario in marriage—when we pledge our commitment to our spouses.

With respect to the word "perform," we perform what we pledge to God that we shall do, and become obligated to do that. It is the same with marriage; when we pledge things to our spouses, we become obligated to perform those pledges.

Finally, with the word "perpetrate," we carry out, or perpetrate -- for example, the act of praying perpetually. Marriages are supposed to be forever, in perpetuity, "until death do us part," but unfortunately, with divorce, it is not always so.

Passion

Praying passionately enhances our relationship with God. Passion also enhances our marriage. When we are passionate in our prayers, we make God our highest priority. It is pertinent now to distinguish all comparisons, similarities, and interrelatedness between prayer and marriage. It should be reiterated that God is first, even before our marriages. God is our highest priority because he is the one who blesses and endorses our marriages, including all the benefits of marriage that follow. The main argument here is that when couples pray together, their marriages are enhanced. Further, some of the benefits of prayers, like intimacy, commitment, and communication with God, that one derives from prayers can be derived in marriages, contingent on couples praying together. Marriage and praying are two different things, but the decisive point is that praying together by spouses binds their marriage together and helps them understand God more.

Passion is important in marriage. Romance and physical unions are also important. Passion is the catalyst that quickens the chemistry of marriage. Passion is like cement that seals the relationship called marriage. It is the glue that binds husband and wife together. The same passion that drives a husband and wife should motivate them to make God their highest priority in marriage and in all their undertakings.

LOVE AND MARRIAGE PERSPECTIVES

Intimacy

A brief explanation is imperative here to enhance the understanding of the arguments that will follow concerning intimacy. Sometimes intimacy can be confusing or misconstrued if not clarified. An intimate relationship with God means knowing God by being close to him. That closeness comes through praying and abiding by the will and commandment of God. Through that closeness, we come to understand God by knowing him and having an intimate association with him. The origin of the word "intimate" is from the Greek, meaning "to know."

In marriage, you have an intimate relationship with your spouse by knowing him or her. That knowing comes from closeness with your spouse, forming the ultimate relationship. Another intimacy in marriage between husband and wife is the sexual union sanctioned by God through marriage between a man and a woman.

An intimate relationship with God is more than having a casual prayer every now and then. It takes a routine, commitment, and dedication to work our way toward knowing God.

Understanding

Prayer enhances our understanding of God. You cannot understand something that you have no knowledge of. There is a saying that to know God is to understand him. Understanding comes with trust and fear of the Lord.

The fear of the Lord is the beginning of knowledge. (Proverbs 1:7)

The fear of the Lord is the beginning of wisdom, and the knowledge of the Holy One is understanding. (Proverbs 9:10)

Trust in the Lord with all your heart and lean not on your own understanding. In all your ways acknowledge him and He shall direct your paths. (Proverbs 3:5–6)

As you trust in the Lord, not only is your understanding of him enhanced, but your ways and paths are further smoothed. Understanding with our spouses enhances our marriages and reduces marital conflicts.

Faithfulness

God wants us to be faithful to him. He made it clear that he is the Lord our God. No other gods or even a likeness of other gods shall be kept.

I am the Lord your God. You shall have no other gods before Me. You shall not make for yourself a carved image—any likeness of anything that is in heaven above, or that is in the earth beneath, or that is in the water under the earth; you shall not bow down to them nor serve them. For I, the Lord your God, am a jealous God, visiting the iniquity of the fa-

thers upon the children to the third and fourth generations of those who hate Me, but showing mercy to thousands, to those who love Me and keep My commandments. (Exodus 20:2–6)

We can be faithful to God by making him a priority in our lives, avoiding temptations in marriage, and not having other gods. In marriage, faithfulness is a key factor that enhances our marriage. Countless marriages have broken up because of unfaithful spouses.

Bonding

Praying helps us bond with God. Bonding with the redeemer is contingent not only on praying but on keeping his commandments as well. Other factors discussed in this interrelatedness, like understanding, faithfulness, intimacy, and so on, enhance bonding with God. The more you keep the commandments of God, the more you bond with him.

If you love me, keep my commandments. (John 14:15)

He who has my commandments and keeps them, it is he who loves Me. And he who loves Me will be loved by My Father, and I will love him and manifest Myself to him. (John 14:21)

Bonding is a two-way street. As you bond with him, he bonds with you. In marriage, bonding is another key element that enhances marriage. The more we bond with our spouses, the smoother the marriage and the more understanding both spouses have.

Conclusion

Praying is important in a marriage relationship. In marriages where spouses do not pray, marriage is like an airplane drifting aimlessly with no pilot, and it will crash in a matter of time. In a marriage where the couples pray, they need to pray continuously. This is vital because when we cease praying, we separate ourselves from God, and once we do that, our marriages become aimless, meaningless, and directionless. A marriage with no focus will head for disaster if not redirected or refocused. That refocusing or redirection is prayer. When we pray in marriage, we ask for petitions needed for a smooth operation of marriage. Those requests include faithfulness, intimacy, understanding, love, bonding, affection, patience, passion, communication, commitment, romance, dedication, devotion, and forgiveness.

If anyone tells you that being prayerful is not important in marriage, I suggest that you talk to someone else. If you do not pray, whom will you call on in time of distress?

> *Hear me when I call, O God of my righteousness. You have relieved me in my distress; have mercy on me and hear my prayer.* (Psalm 4:1)

LOVE AND MARRIAGE PERSPECTIVES

Your attitude in prayers matters. We should be humble and show humility. When we ask God for something, we should have confidence.

> *Now this is the confidence that we have in Him, that if we ask anything according to His will, He hears us. And if we know that He hears us, whatever we ask, we know that we have the petitions that we have asked of Him.* (I John 5:14–15)

Inviting God into your marriage through prayers

Marriage consists exclusively of two people. Any other person coming into the marriage or even attempting to come in is intruding. Christian marriage, however, technically consists of three figures. In a Christian marriage, both spouses make a collective decision to invite a third person into their marriage. That third person is God. By inviting God into the marriage, the couple is asking for guidance, wanting God to help them in directing the affairs of the marriage. It does not necessarily mean that the couple is having problems in the marriage, but you may want to ask, who never has problems in their marriage? Whether the spouses are having problems or not, it makes tremendous sense to want to invite God into your marriage, due to the simple fact that you never know when you will need that help.

Individual relationships with God

People have their personal or individual relationships with God, and each person is responsible for his or her own relationship with God. People's needs and wants are unique and individual, and people feel that they can relate better to God when they are alone in their prayers. Some are shy and feel that this inhibits them; therefore, they pray alone. Others feel that it is distracting having someone else around, for they want to have that deep concentration and to relate to God in the manner that they deem appropriate. People's styles of praying are different, and God reaches people in different ways, depending on what is asked of him and the circumstances involved. That being the case, why is it necessary for spouses to pray together?

Why should spouses pray together?

The answer to this unique question is complicated yet simple. In marriage, a man and a woman come together to become husband and wife. Through that union of matrimony, they become one flesh. This unique oneness gives them same hopes, dreams, and aspirations, as well as shared problems that may arise during the marriage. After this union, their problems are neither the wife's nor the husband's but theirs together. Remember that the husband and wife complement each other. The husband's success is also the wife's success, and vice versa. It does not matter which particular spouse achieved which success. Since they share common problems, it makes perfect sense to pray together for those successes as well as failures or anything else that the couple wants or needs. Praying together enhances communication between spouses because it helps to know how to relate to each other. Imagine one spouse telling the other, "Honey, go and pray while I cook breakfast. By the way, tell God that I still need a job so I can help you pay the rent." How do you think God would react to that kind of prayer, assuming you call that a prayer? I am not trying to teach anyone who believes differently on how to pray here, but there is a right way to pray. Spouses should pray with their emotions. The point of stating that is to illustrate the emotions, feelings, and mutual give-and-take involved in prayers. If those elements are involved, they are also involved in marriage, if you think about it. Spouses are already deeply rooted in those things and are uniquely designed to incorporate those in their prayers and communications with God.

Spiritual significances

The key to praying in marriage situations depends on the way we present our petition before God, for it is stated as follows:

And those who seek me diligently will find me. (Proverbs 8:17)

As couples, the initial thing we need to do is to find how to seek him, how we present our prayers to him, and the timing of our emotions and our affect at the time of praying matters. Our

PRAYER AND MARRIAGE

devotion is also important, as is the way we communicate our prayers to God.

> *Ask, and it will be given to you; seek, and you will find; knock, and it will be opened to you. For everyone who asks receives, and he who seeks finds, and to him who knocks it will be opened.* (Matthew 7:7–8)

God opened his heart up to couples by showing his compassion, for he will give if we ask, and we shall receive if we ask. Praying is a two-way street—and so is communication. God gave spouses direct access when he stated that communication would be opened. That opening is contingent upon couples knocking, which is equivalent to seeking him diligently. God essentially gave spouses a choice that he is available if we seek, want, and need him. So couples seeking God's guidance in their marriage are also making a decision. In this book, we talked about love being a choice and a decision. If we can make the choice and decision to be in love, we can also make the decision to seek God in marriage. They are all interwoven.

> *For where your treasure is, there is your heart also.* (Matthew 6:21)

I can almost assure you that most people's minds and hearts are on their marriages. If your mind or heart is not on your marriage, why did you marry that person? By the same token and reasoning, if your marriage is not your treasure, you may have married for the wrong reasons. As part of a couple, your marriage is your heart, and your heart is your marriage; it then follows that you should work hard to keep your treasure. Anything valuable, we keep in prayers. We pray when our children get sick; we pray when we need a new car or a promotion on the job; we pray so that we will not be fired from our jobs; and we pray whenever we get in any kind of trouble. If we pray for all those things, why can't we then pray for our marriages? If we start prioritizing things that are important in our lives, marriage should be one of those things at the top of the list, so why not pray for it?

"When two or three are gathered together in my name, I shall grant their request." So it was said in the Bible. God continues to lure couples by giving those directives on what to do. In simplified language, a husband and a wife meet the criteria of "two or three are gathered together." Again, all we have to do as a couple is ask. To show you how things are simplified for us, God already knows our needs even before we ask. Since all we have to do is ask, we as spouses will be failing in our marriages if we do not ask. Spouses can start reading the scriptures together. As they read, they can verbally discuss their understandings of the scriptures. If they prefer to write it down, they can do so separately to see what each thinks and get together to compare and process their notes. In processing their notes, they are also sharing their feelings about the scriptures and their innermost feelings. Such an exercise helps to understand each other's thought process in certain situations. Those understandings foster their understandings of their marital relationship. This will enhance a relationship based on love and trust. Marital discord is reduced to the barest minimum.

As we pray together, our faith in God and in our marriages is enhanced. Consider the following:

> *But let him ask in faith, with no doubting, for he who doubts is like a wave of the sea driven and tossed by the wind.* (James 1:6)

There is a correlation between having faith in God and having faith in our marriage. Having faith in God not only helps faith in our marriages, but also faith in ourselves. Faith is inside of us, and what is inside of us always reflects outside of us. With faith in us, God, and marriage, we act in unison and should be able to conquer most of the temptations and misunderstandings inherent in marriage. I want to reiterate that the family that prays together stays together. Being in a Christian marriage does not instantly guarantee marital success. Marriage has its difficulties, and our faith will continue to be tested. Marriage is one area where patience and understanding reign supreme. Patience is also paramount in praying, as we will see below.

Patience is paramount in praying

You would be amazed how many couples pray to God in the morning and expect their answer from God by afternoon. Some also pray only when they need God's assistance and cease praying once their prayers are answered. In the scripture, we are told to pray without ceasing. In the first Epistle of Paul the Apostle to Timothy, the issue of prayer was advocated and desired:

> *I desire therefore that the men pray everywhere, lifting up holy hands, without wrath and doubting.* (I Timothy 2:8)

The importance of prayer in our daily lives and in marriage cannot be overstated.

When they pray, some couples feel that their prayers are not being answered soon enough, and they throw in the towel and quit praying. In the Epistle of James, we learn what could come with our patience and faith:

> *My brethren, count it all joy when you fall into various trials, knowing that the testing of your faith produces patience. But let patience have its perfect work, that you may be perfect and complete, lacking nothing.* (James 1:2-4)

From the preceding, as you may have noticed, we need patience when we pray. We continue asking God for things but do not wait sometimes to put in the dedication and work for our prayers to be answered. It is like being in a marriage but not wanting to put in the work and patience needed for our marriages to succeed. The scripture quoted above also talks about testing our faith. As I stated previously in this book, God continues to test us and our faith. It could be God's test of faith to see where we are as couples before answering our prayers or granting our requests. The next quotation shows what happens when we have that patience and faith:

> *If any of you lacks wisdom, let him ask of God, who gives to all liberally and without reproach, and it will be given to him.* (James 1:5)

When God gives, he gives liberally and without reproach. This type of giving is not automatic. Remember that we have to do our part as couples, by following Christ's ways and asking, of course. As we ask and have ongoing communication with God through prayers, he knows at what point in time to grant our requests. I mentioned following Christ's ways in this paragraph. What does that mean? Let us explore the answers below.

Following Christ's ways

There was a woman that I was trying to impress years ago. We went to church together, and I heard two songs: "I Have Decided to Follow Jesus," and "What a Friend We Have in Jesus." I never knew the significance of those two songs until years later. I ran across a hymnbook and read the words of those songs, and that's when it dawned on me. The scripture told us of when some misunderstanding came about the commandments of God and Jesus was asked which the first commandment of all is. He answered as follows:

LOVE AND MARRIAGE PERSPECTIVES

> *"The first of all the commandments is: 'Hear, O Israel, the Lord our God, the Lord is one. And you shall love the Lord your God with all your heart, with all your soul, with all your mind, and with all your strength. This is the first commandment. And the second, like it, is this: 'You shall love your neighbor as yourself.' There is no other commandment greater than these."* (Mark 12:29–31)

There seems to be no reason to add anything else, for this says it all. Love God first, and then love your neighbor as yourself. That is following Christ's ways. Remember that your spouse is also your neighbor, and you should love him or her as well. Christ demonstrated to us how to live, by being humble and sensitive to the needs of others. In so doing, we share God's love among each other.

Finally, we should approach God with spirit of humility, repentance, forgiveness, homage, and contrition. In marriage, we need his compassionate mercy and his redemptive tenderness. As couples, we should make prayer a vital importance in our lives. Praying is our most cherished treasure as we seek friendship with Jesus. As we pray in marriage, we ask God to guide our families and us from deceptions, temptations, distractions, and delusions of this world. We further ask and pray that he will help our marriages, guide, protect, and make us loving couples so that we can live happily ever after. I now leave you, the reader of this book, with a thought to ponder:

PRAYER AND MARRIAGE

Praying always with all prayer and supplication in the Spirit, being watchful to this end with all perseverance and supplication for all the saints. (Ephesians 6:18)

Prayer helps define and strengthen family relationships. Husbands and wives should set a specific time of day to share their reflections. This serves two purposes. First, it draws husbands and wives closer together so they can love themselves more and share their love for one another. Second, it draws the whole family closer in God's love, thereby directing the family to the right path of life. Prayer nourishes the heart and mind, thereby developing a conjugal and family spirituality. It reminds children about the priorities in life and is also mindful of eternal life. Remember that in life there are the following things, according to Cameron (2000, 18): "Joys and sorrows, hopes and disappointments, births and birthday celebrations, wedding anniversaries of parents or our own, departures, separations, and homecomings, important and far-reaching decisions, the deaths of who are dear, etc.—all of these mark God's loving intervention in the family's history. They should be seen as suitable moments for thanksgiving, for petition, for trusting abandonment of the family into the hands of their common father in heaven."

There is a vast difference between saying prayers and praying.

—Unknown

CHAPTER TEN

Marital Stress

Stress is when you wake up screaming and you realize you haven't fallen asleep yet.
—Unknown

STRESS IS PART of life, and it is everywhere. It is in our jobs, relationships, marriages, and in our daily activities. It does not discriminate. No age, social class, gender, ethnicity, or educational background is immune to stress. There is also stress among Christians, including husbands and wives.

Stress affects our minds, bodies, and souls. If you are affected by stress, some people regard you as weak-minded. That is a myth. Stress should be taken seriously and should be treated, just as we would any other disorder. Any person with stress symptomatology should seek adequate intervention, for it does not just disappear on its own. If stress is ignored, it can have a harmful effect on that individual. It can lead to further deterioration of the body. Stress is internalized through the mind. When the body perceives a stressful situation, it reacts to it. The more stress the body perceives, the greater the intensity of reaction the body emits. Stress is progressive, and it is appropriate to review its progression.

LOVE AND MARRIAGE PERSPECTIVES

Progression of stress

Stress can begin in many ways. As stress manifests and progresses, it starts from the lower to moderate and progresses to the highest level. The range of progression depends on the spectrum that the stress was at prior to intervention. Stress can start with headaches, insomnia, poor concentration, helplessness, hopelessness, and phobias, all of which are worrisome and depressive symptomatology. It can progress to anger, aggression, and addictive behaviors like drug use, overeating, sex addiction, and other compulsive disorders. Further progression includes hypertension (high blood pressure), strokes, heart attacks, elevated blood sugar levels, migraine headaches, muscle spasms, increased heart palpitations, and even death.

I hope that this progressive ladder illustrates the seriousness of stress as well as the imperativeness of spouses seeking appropriate intervention. Treating stress should not be avoided, though unfortunately some couples use avoidance technique as a way of dealing with stress. Other spouses deal with stress by ignoring, distracting, suppressing, or repressing. In some chapters, we discussed having plans to deal with issues affecting marriages. Likewise, we should be familiar with stress symptomatology and have a mechanism in place to deal with it if it strikes. The key to stress in marriage is having the necessary coping skills to manage the stress and help alleviate stressors.

MARITAL STRESS

Origin of stress in marriage

It all started in that garden called Eden, when Adam and Eve ate the fruit of knowledge that God had forbidden them to eat. Let us briefly review Adam and Eve's situation before this debacle of fruit eating. Adam and his wife, Eve, were living a stress-free life. God provided everything they needed and wanted. They were living in a paradise, and none of the luxuries and amenities of their time were lacking. They were given power and access to everything except that particular tree, so stress was out of the question.

Can you imagine being in a place where all your needs are taken care of? You do not have to worry about paying rent or a mortgage. You have food and clothing. You have no need for money, and you have no bills; you just enjoy and live a stress-free life. Such was the situation with the first couple, Adam and Eve, until they ate they forbidden fruit of knowledge.

Why, Eve, why?

If they saw Eve today, some couples might want to ask her why she ate that fruit of knowledge. The question seems pertinent because Eve had everything that she needed: a devoted husband, prestige, attention from God, power, respect, and no stress. She had no worries, pressures, or concerns. Nothing could compare to her situation. She even had dominion over everything, including animals, plants, birds of the air, and fishes of the sea. As you

LOVE AND MARRIAGE PERSPECTIVES

may have noticed, Eve was okay with her life until she started comparing herself with God, believing that if she ate the fruit, she would be like God.

Since Eve had everything going for her before this incident, that is why it seems prudent to ask her why she did what she did. Before we get to the answers, note that as spouses, we tend to blame each other for things that happen in the marriage instead of accepting responsibility for our behaviors or actions. Adam even blamed Eve when he said the following:

> *The woman whom you gave to be with me, she gave me of the tree, and I ate.* (Genesis 3:12)

Adam might not have been cursed if he had not rationalized his actions or projected blame to his spouse and instead had the spirit of repentance and contrition. Perhaps he should have told God that as the head of the family, he accepted responsibility for his actions by eating the fruit of the tree—that he also accepted responsibility for his wife's actions: her giving him the fruit that he accepted. "Lord," Adam should probably have continued, "I was disobedient by eating the fruit of the tree, and I sincerely ask for your compassionate mercy and forgiveness. If you by chance forgive me, Lord, I will ensure that I will not make the same mistake, and I will discuss this issue with Eve." Being compassionate, God probably would have forgiven Adam. The curse that followed him "all the days of his life" (Genesis 3:18) perhaps could have been avoided. If that particular curse had been avoided, our situation as descendants of Adam and Eve might be different today.

Comparative Advantage in Marriage

As spouses, we need to accept responsibility for our behavior and actions. The moment we start blaming our spouses, we are unknowingly injecting stress into our marriages. Furthermore, we are being judgmental instead of controlling our own behavior. As couples, we should find ways to de-stress our marriages instead of stressing them. We can achieve this by being who we are, the person God created each of us to be, rather than trying to be someone else. Trying to be like someone else does nothing but bring stress to a marriage. We keep comparing ourselves with other couples to see who is more beautiful, has a bigger house, has more money, has a better job, and has better grandchildren. All these comparisons are stress-related. I will elaborate more on this phenomenon, which I call the theory of comparative advantage.

Back to Eve -- for the couples who want to ask Eve why she did what she did, that might be rather judgmental. It is human nature that Eve ate the fruit of the tree that she was forbidden to eat. Adam and Eve disobeyed God, and as spouses, we should not disobey God. Do you know the amount of stress that we bring into our marriages when we disobey God? We disobey God and then wonder why our marriages are stressed. We brought that stress into our marriages, and here is how we can eliminate it:

Rule #1: Understand that in marriage, our actions precipitate stress, and our actions can alleviate stress as well.

Rule #2: Accept blame or responsibility for our actions in marriage to decrease stress, and understand that blaming our spouses for our actions increases stress.

Effect of Adam and Eve's actions

Adam and Eve paid dearly for their disobedience and brought wanton repercussions and stress on themselves and mankind. God cursed them, and that curse, some argue, continues on other spouses even today. Adam and Eve lost their home, or paradise, so to speak. Can you imagine the devastation in losing your home as a couple? How about the stress of paying your mortgage or your rent? They were homeless, and with homelessness, came despair. They even realized that they were naked and had to make their own clothing, something that they were not used to.

> *Then the eyes of both of them were opened, and they knew that they were naked; and they sewed fig leaves together and made themselves coverings.* (Genesis 3:7)

Can you imagine the stress of doing something that you are not used to doing, plus the added stress of doing it for the first time? The problem that Eve had never manifested until she was deceived by Satan into comparing herself with God. The serpent confused her into believing that a different situation was better than what she had. In marriage, some have the same problem: not appreciating what they have, thinking that what other couples have is better. What we fail to realize is that God created each couple differently, and they have their own unique gifts and talents from God.

Rule #3: Do not compare or wish to be like other couples, for comparisons in marriage lead to stress. God has a plan for each couple. There is a time and place for everything. You will have yours when your time comes.

Sometimes in marriage, we do not even know when God has blessed us. It is human nature to think that the grass is always greener on the other side of the fence. Adam and Eve had everything in their marriage but lost it trying to be something other than what God made them to be. They were uniquely blessed but failed to realize it.

Rule #4: In marriage, always be content with what God gave you. Your husband or wife is a gift from God, as are your children. You can be missing your unique blessings by not realizing how abundantly you are blessed until that blessing is taken away.

Before their eviction from the Garden of Eden, Adam had a special relationship with God, which was why he and Eve had everything at their disposal. Adam lost that special relationship with God, and his life became stressful and traumatic thereafter.

LOVE AND MARRIAGE PERSPECTIVES

Rule #5: As a couple, strive to have a relationship with God. Do not come to God only when you are stressed with your petitions and wondering why your prayers are not answered sometimes. The reason Adam was hiding from God was because his special relationship with God was irretrievably broken. God no longer perceived them the way he used to. Adam and Eve even saw themselves differently, prompting their shame and causing them to hide from God when they heard his voice. Genesis 3:8–11 illustrates it vividly:

> *And they heard the sound of the Lord God walking in the garden in the cool of the day, and Adam and his wife hid themselves from the presence of the Lord God among the trees of the garden. Then the Lord God called to Adam and said to him, "Where are you?" So he said, "I heard Your voice in the garden, and I was afraid because I was naked...." And He said, "Have you eaten from the tree of which I commanded you that you should not eat?"*

Adam was an intelligent man. Adam knew that they sinned when they ran away from God. As we sin, we become separated from God. It is a fearful thing not to be with God or on the side of God. Fear is very stressful and distressing, for it signifies a probable danger. The preparation we make to deal with that danger is stressful. The lack of preparation is also stressful. As couples, we should avoid things that will lead us to fear, thereby reducing one more stress in our marriages. As Christians, we also know what the wages of sin is as stated in the Bible. We inherited our sinful nature from Adam and Eve. This sinful nature causes stress in our marriages, and as spouses that affects us tremendously.

Stress in marriage

In researching this book, I came across several definitions of marriage. It became conclusive that one's definition of marriage sometimes has to do with his experiences in marriage, or at least his perceptions of it. The following definitions of marriage tend to suggest someone who perhaps had a stressful marriage. Morley (1994) gave some definitions of marriage from different sources, and here are some of them. In the fourth century BC, Meander defines marriage the following way:

"Marriage is an evil that most men welcome." —Mowstikoi

"Marriage is a desperate thing." —John Seldon, seventh century

"Marriage is like a life—it is a field of battle, not a bed of roses." —Robert Louis Stevenson, nineteenth century

"Marriage happens as with cages: the birds without despair to get in, and those within despair of getting out." —Montaigne, sixteenth century

Having defined marriage from a stressful perspective, let us now discuss what triggers stress in marriage.

LOVE AND MARRIAGE PERSPECTIVES

Stress triggers in marriage

We encounter stress in our everyday interactions with others. Sometimes as spouses, we bring these stressors home. In marriage, our actions and behavior are a precursor to stress. We may not want to accept that most couples tend to blame each other for their stressors instead of accepting responsibility for their actions. Even Adam blamed Eve for what happened in Eden.

Several factors trigger stress in marriages. Some of these factors include the following: yourself, your spouse, peer pressure, sickness, financial problems, children, status of employment, sexual issues, life changes, drinking or substance abuse, fear of failure, fear of the unknown, not following God's teachings, the possibility of divorce, and so on. Let us address some of these factors.

Yourself

The chief stressor in your marriage is yourself, but please do not be angry at me for stating it that way. The reason that you are the chief stressor is that you can control your own self, behavior, and actions. It is human nature to project blame, rationalize, and focus our actions or behaviors on others instead of accepting responsibility. In marriages, that other is your significant other—your spouse. We sometimes project and blame him or her for things that happen in the marriage. We make the issues provisional or contingent on our spouse such as "If he or she had not done such and such, I would not have reacted the way I did."

MARITAL STRESS

On the other hand, if your spouse does exactly what you want, your response may be that he or she should have done it differently, and that was why you were angry. If you look at the above scenarios, you are still blaming. Why not accept that you were angry and apologize for being angry? With your acceptance and apology, you have relieved yourself and your spouse of the stress. You may want to ask yourself, *What about my spouse's action and behavior in all this?* Exploring that issue is going to complicate the situation and inject more stress into this issue. Why is that so? Let us examine that.

You are responsible for your own behavior, and your spouse is responsible for his or her own behavior. If you take responsibility for your behavior and he or she takes responsibility for his or her actions, there is no further stress. The stress continues when we tend to pass blame back and forth, for nothing is resolved that way.

Rule #6: Know that you are responsible for your actions, and your spouse is responsible for his or her actions. Accepting responsibility for your actions de-stresses the marriage. Projecting or assigning blame to your spouse increases stress in marriage.

Rule #7: When it comes to relieving stress in marriage, remember that the only behavior you can control is yours. Attempting to control your spouse's behavior takes the focus away from you.

LOVE AND MARRIAGE PERSPECTIVES

Your Spouse

Of all the factors, this will be the shortest issue to discuss. It was designed that way so both husband and wife know about individual responsibility for their actions. It is further designed to ensure that there should be no blaming, rationalizing, or projecting by either spouse. What applies to your spouse applies to you.

Peer pressure

This can be a big stressor. The couple that you know across town has a big house; you want one. Your neighbor has a new car; you want one. In wanting those things that your neighbor and the couple across town have, did you take into account their situation and yours? Why did they get a big house? How many people do they have in the family? Are their in-laws or other family members moving in? What if their grown children and grandchildren are moving in because of certain circumstances? Did they come by an inheritance or even win the lottery? Now that you all of a sudden have a desire for a bigger house, how will you pay that mortgage? How stable is your job and that of your spouse? At the time of this writing, many homes have foreclosed because of the downward spiral in the economy. Can you imagine the stress of the couples foreclosing, not to mention what their children are going through? The reason for mentioning this is that sometimes couples let their peers influence them instead of making their own decisions. If there is no forethought, this will lead to stress for the couple wanting a bigger house. Doing something like buying a house because another couple did is adding stress to your marriage.

Rule #8: Do not let the actions of other couples influence your marriage. Letting other people influence your marriage is stressful. Be yourself and not somebody else.

Sickness

Sickness is a stressor in marriage. Can you imagine the amount of stress a spouse goes through if the other spouse is sick? The degree of stress increases with the intensity of the sickness. When one spouse, let us assume the husband, is sick, that will stress the wife. The children are also stressed by their father's sickness. Can you now imagine how the stress will devastate the family if the husband is the major breadwinner and is unable to go to work, but has no sick time accrued or disability benefits? Bills will fall behind, which affects the couple's credit rating. What type of stress do you think the wife will have in going to her own job and caring for her sick husband plus her children, not to mention other domestic issues that warrant her attention? The stress level for the wife and the rest of the family will be high.

Sickness has the potential of making marital relationships stronger or weaker. They can become stronger in the sense that in the above scenario, for example, the wife can show the depth of her love in how she cares for her husband during his sickness. The husband knows firmly by the virtue of his wife's care that he can depend on her in time of need, thereby strengthening their relationship. Following the same scenario illustrated above, the wife can decide that she does not want to stay in the marriage any longer and use the sickness as an excuse to leave. That is an example of how sickness can weaken or even end a marriage. Stories abound about some spouses leaving their marriages when the other spouse falls sick, especially with debilitating illnesses. These actions and situations stress marriages.

Financial problems

Paying bills is stressful, and it is even more stressful when you do not have the money for those bills. Financial problems in marriage are devastating. Your children may need things that you do not have the financial capability to provide. Remember, as I stated in this chapter, that our actions in marriage precipitate stress. In marriage, we need to prioritize our needs in order of importance, starting with food, and our rent or mortgage, which should be at the top of the list. We need to learn how to manage our money to minimize our financial problems. The more mechanisms we have as couples to manage our money, the less the marriage will be stressful. I do not like money, but I like what money can buy. The fact that I like what money can buy does not mean that I should live above my means, nor should married couples. The rash of foreclosures going on during the writing of this book illustrates how some couples living above their means bought houses that they cannot afford. Not living within their means stressed their marriages and resulted in their homes being foreclosed.

Rule #9: Live within your means. Living above your means brings untold financial problems and stresses your marriage even more.

Children

Children can stress marriages in different ways. I will discuss only two here. First is when a couple is trying to have children but for one reason or another cannot have any. I have seen couples go through their life savings in their attempts to have a child, and sometimes with no success. The couples go through the added stress of wondering what they did wrong. Depending on the strength of their faith, they may feel like questioning God as to why other couples have children and they can't. If their relationship is not strong enough, one can start blaming the other as to whose fault it is that they did not have a child. Marriages can even fail.

Second, there are the couples who do have children, and their stress is a result of the behaviors or actions of the children. This stress is magnified at the adolescent stage, when children have the potential for acting out problems. Sometimes children at that age have compulsive behaviors like experimenting with drugs and sex. These are tremendous stressors for parents. Those behaviors can result in addiction or legal problems, further compounding stress. This buttresses the point for us to be actively involved with our children. This involvement can inhibit or nip issues as stated above before they even start. Again, in marriage, our actions precipitate stress. If we as parents fail to supervise our children adequately, the fault is on us. Our children are our future, and it is up to us to instill discipline in them so they can do the same for their own children.

Status of employment

During my adolescent years, I overheard my father discussing with my mother the possibility of his being laid off from his job. They were not aware that I overheard that conversation. My father was the only one working at that time. I was old enough to understand then that people make money only when they go to work. Despite my young age at the time, I felt my heart stop beating for a second. Passing by, I could tell from the look on my mother's face that she was worried about the possibility of her husband being laid off. Now an adult and faced with potential unstable employment myself sometimes, I realize that my parents were experiencing a lot of stress then.

Can you imagine you and your spouse facing probable lack of employment in your own marriage? I am sure that would stress any couple. In marriage, it is always good to have plans and save for a rainy day in case there is a sudden loss of employment. One might argue that some couples barely make enough to have some left over for savings. That is so true. The point of the matter is that all these mentioned situations concerning employment can stress marriages. These stressors are compounded if a spouse is laid off and doesn't qualify for unemployment benefits. The result is unwanted stress for the marriage and family.

Sexual issues

Two areas concerning sexual issues can lead to stress in marriage. First is lack of sexual satisfaction. Second is infidelity, cheating by one or both spouses in marriage. Let us address the first one. Lack of sexual satisfaction in marriage can mean different things for different couples. To some, it could mean not getting enough sex. To others, it could mean lack of performance by either spouse. Regardless of which is the case, it can stress the marriage when either spouse thinks that the sex is not what it was intended to be. Such issues could be resolved by the spouses discussing the problem. During this discussion, the couple should be honest with each other by discussing the type of sex that each person wants. You would be amazed how things can be worked out with honest negotiation and discussion. On the other hand, there could be erectile dysfunction problems that may warrant pharmacological intervention. Such discussions are stress relievers, giving each couple information about each other.

Regarding the second issue, in respect to unfaithfulness by one or both spouses, three things need to be ironed out.

LOVE AND MARRIAGE PERSPECTIVES

(a) Is the cheating a result of issues that happened in the marriage?

(b) Is the cheating a result of one spouse cheating just for the sake of cheating?

(c) Is the cheating because the other spouse is getting even? In other words if he can cheat, she can cheat also. However, in either scenario, cheating by any spouse is wrong and stressful.

A spouse may cheat because he or she is not getting sexual satisfaction in the marriage. The cheating spouse does not intend to divorce the spouse, or so it seems. He or she tends to rationalize the affair by verbalizing the intactness of the family. What the cheating spouse is doing is removing the focus from his or her cheating and at the same time presenting the persona of being a family-oriented person. The cheating spouses always forget that the logic for the defense of their behavior never adds up. Before any spouse cheats, he or she should think how that action is going to impact the marriage and the family. The stress of that behavior is monumental to the marriage.

The other examples are when a spouse is cheating for the sake of cheating, and when another spouse cheats to get even. No type of cheating is good in any marriage; two wrongs do not make things right. Rampant cheating needs therapeutic intervention. It is even safer to state that *any* cheating warrants therapeutic intervention, especially when there is a lack of remorse and probability of that behavior being repeated. Cheating is not only bad, but immoral. Every book in the scripture condemns it.

Compulsive drinking

Compulsive drinking definitely stresses marriage. A marriage where one spouse or both are alcoholics influences the marriage negatively. Let us look at a scenario where the husband is the drinker. There is the probability that being an alcoholic, he can miss going to work some days. That is less income to the family. Bills will perpetually be behind because of less money that he brings in. No matter how little income he has, he spends it on alcohol. The marriage and the family take a backseat, and the drinking becomes the dominant theme in his life. That type of behavior and the result of the drinking is a stressor in the marriage. There is always the threat of eviction or foreclosure due to instability in the rent or mortgage payment. There is always the looming danger of health problems associated with excessive drinking. Cirrhosis of the liver and other related health issues come to mind. If any of these health problems occurred, can you imagine the stress level and financial impact on the marriage?

Prior to this stage, it would be a good idea for the wife to suggest therapeutic intervention. Most typical alcoholics have denial issues, so the stress of convincing him to enter a treatment program could take a toll. If he did agree to go to a treatment program, there could be financial obligations that the family may not be able to meet. This would further complicate a complicated problem, leading to added stress for the wife and the marriage. Then there is the strong possibility that the husband could go back to drinking after recovering from his sickness. This exposes him to further health deterioration and more stress in the marriage.

Fear of failure and fear of the unknown

There is always the fear that a marriage can end in divorce or that things can go wrong in the marriage. This fear adds to the stress in marriage. Concerning fear of divorce, any spouse who takes care of his or her responsibilities should not have that phobia. By this, I mean that if you follow the dictates of your wedding vows, and your spouse follows his/hers, there is a strong possibility that the marriage will be fine. Each spouse is an adult and can therefore discern between right and wrong. So trust in God and do the right thing.

Let us now review stresses arising in marriage due to not following God or his teachings.

God's teachings

Words in the scripture aid in stress management. Following the scripture is also a way to avoid stress. When God made us in his own image, he knew what we needed in order to have stress-free lives. All we have to do is follow God's teachings in order to have less stressful lives and marriages. He had a plan for Adam and Eve, but they did not follow God's plan. He also has a plan for us.

> *"For I know well the plans I have in mind for you," says the Lord, "plans for your welfare, not for woe. Plans to give you a future full of hope, when you call me, when you go pray to me, I will listen to you. When you look for me, you will find me. Yes, when you seek me with all your heart you will find me with you, says the Lord."* (Jeremiah 29:11–13, NAB)

Rule #10: Realize that the more we follow God's teachings and his plan, the less stress we have. The less we follow God's teachings and his plan, the more stress we have. It is said in the scripture:

> *Let not your heart be troubled; you believe in God, believe also in me. In My Father's house are many mansions; if it were not so, I would have told you. I go to prepare a place for you. And if I go and prepare a place for you, I will come again and receive you to myself; that where I am, there you may be also. And where I go you know, and the way you know.* (John 14:1–4)

As you ruminate on the above saying, consider the quote below.

> *Abide in Me, and I in you. As the branch cannot bear fruit of itself, unless it abides in the vine, neither can you, unless you abide in Me. I am the vine, you are the branches. He who*

abides in Me, and I in him, bears much fruit; for without me you can do nothing. If anyone does not abide in Me, he is cast out as a branch and is withered; and they gather them and throw them into the fire, and they are burned. If you abide in Me, and my words abide in you, you will ask what you desire, and it shall be done for you. (John 15:4–7)

If we follow God's teachings but are still stressed in marriage and in our lives, he will save us in the same way he saved Jacob from his distress. Remember that to be saved from that distress, all we have to do is believe:

How mighty is that day—none like it. A time of distress for Jacob, though he shall be saved from it. (Jeremiah 30:7, NAB)

Jacob shall again find rest, shall be tranquil and undisturbed, for I am with you, says the Lord, to deliver you. (Jeremiah 30:10–11, NAB)

As a couple, having a relationship with God will save us lots of stress. When we experience stress, we should seek solace with God, for he said that we should come to him as follows:

Come to me, all you who labor and are burdened, and I will give you rest. Take my yoke upon you and learn from me, for I am meek and humble of heart; and you will find rest for yourselves. (Matthew 11:28–29, NAB)

Managing stress God's way

There is nothing like the spirit of God and guidance from God. Regardless of our stress in marriage, we should prevail, overcoming that stress and being peaceful. The key to overcoming that stress is to believe and have faith in God. Human nature is overridden by God's spirit. As stated previously, our actions precipitate stress in our marriage. God's influence and power in our lives give us the ability to view our actions differently, compared to what we are able to see if God is not in our lives to influence and direct us. This inner peace and God's guidance are contingent on following his will. When he was stressed prior to being betrayed, Jesus still followed the will of His Father:

> *Abba, Father, all things are possible for You. Take this cup away from me; nevertheless, not what I will but what You will.* (Mark 14:36)

Viewing things from God's perspective is comforting because we know that we are on God's side. The Psalm of David illustrates this:

> *Yea, though I walk through the valley of the shadow of death, I will fear no evil, for You are with me. Your rod and Your staff, they comfort me.* (Psalm 23:4)

God's spirit is more powerful than anything we can think of. That is why we need God's spirit all the time in our marriages and in

LOVE AND MARRIAGE PERSPECTIVES

dealings with others. When God's love is in our hearts, it controls everything in us. God's love teaches us how to empathize with others at all times, especially when those people are in distress. God's peace comes from him. Nothing can substitute God's peace. By giving our marriages to God, we have that peacefulness and understanding. Through God's peace, we have to believe that this is possible and sincerely seek that peace through God. That comes with petition, prayers, and supplication.

> *Be anxious for nothing, but in everything by prayer and supplication, with thanksgiving, let your requests be made known to God; and the peace of God, which surpasses all understanding, will guard your hearts and minds through Christ Jesus.* (Philippians 4:6–7)

God is peace. In our marriages, if we find God, we've found peace. It is stated in John 16:33, NAB:

> *You might have peace in me. In the world you will have trouble, but take courage, I have conquered the world.*

Concluding the discussion on God's peace, I leave you with the following:

> *Peace I leave with you, My peace I give to you; not as the world gives do I give to you. Let not your heart be troubled, neither let it be afraid.* (John 14:27)

Temptations versus stress

I will end this chapter with temptation in marriage, for temptation leads to marital stress. The way we as couples react to that temptation can stress the marriage. If the devil can tempt the Lord Jesus Christ, nobody and no marriage is immune from his temptation. When temptation comes in marriages, couples have to resist that temptation. Christ resisted his temptation by letting the devil know this:

> *It is written again, "You shall not tempt the Lord your God." (Matthew 4:7)*

That resistance comes with a marriage plan and maturity. Without maturity and without following God's plan, we create our own circumstances. Some spouses' lack of maturity lets them yield to the temptation of sex outside the marriage. As mature people, we should live life on its own terms. Following a defined marriage plan that both spouses agreed to helps in successful achievement of marriage and life goals. As we achieve our marriage goals, we also achieve what God ultimately destined for us. Regarding this maturity and attaining our goals, it is said in Philippians 3:14–16:

> *I press toward the goal for the prize of the upward call of God in Christ Jesus. Therefore let us, as many as are mature, have this mind; and if in anything you think otherwise, God will reveal even this to you. Nevertheless, to the degree that*

LOVE AND MARRIAGE PERSPECTIVES

we have already attained, let us walk by the same rule, let us be of the same mind.

Maturity is not reacting to our feelings and emotions impulsively. This includes thinking things out before acting, regardless of the pressure. Maturity is being accountable and responsible to our spouses. This accountability trickles down to our children and the way we relate to others. Being responsible for our own actions, we should resist any urge to go against our marriage vows and things that will stress our spouses and marriages. Consider these closing thoughts:

Now therefore, listen to me, my children, for blessed are those who keep my ways. Hear instruction and be wise, and do not disdain it. Blessed is the man who listens to me, watching daily at my gates, waiting at the posts of my doors. For whoever finds me finds life, and obtains favor from the Lord; but he who sins against me wrongs his own soul; all those who hate me love death. (Proverbs 8:32–36)

Adopting the right attitude can convert a negative stress into a positive one.

—Hans Selye

CHAPTER ELEVEN

Anger In Marriage

When angry, count to ten before you speak; if very angry, a hundred.

—Thomas Jefferson

ANGER IS THE inability to handle frustrating situations. It is also an emotional reaction to hostility that brings personal displeasure either to us or to someone else. In other words, anger is a feeling. Anger is something we express. Further, anger is something we can manage.

Even though anger is a feeling, some see it as a feeling of displeasure. However, a person expressing anger can channel it into a positive anger, like in a grieving process where the family of a deceased member requests that you donate to a charity in lieu of flowers.

Anger is usually negative. In that instance, the person expressing the anger may choose to channel it into negative anger by expressing it in destructive ways. Anger can lead to aggressive behavior if not expressed appropriately. The individual expressing anger can also be in a state of rage with his or her unhealthy expression of anger. The key to anger is the way you express it.

Whether positive or negative, anger impacts marriage.

Anger expression

Anger can wreak havoc in our marriages if not appropriately expressed or addressed. It can further affect our mental health if we do not gain control of it. Anger is a necessary emotion. It is a signal to the angry person that something is wrong with the marriage relationship or the environment of the marriage. Anger can empower or be disempowering, depending on the issues and circumstances, but above all the ability or inability of couples to channel their anger. Anger can be constructive in marriage if expressed appropriately or destructive if expressed inappropriately. Let us review constructive and destructive anger—and how each relates to marriage.

What constructive and destructive anger means

Constructive, appropriate, and healthy expressions of anger will be used interchangeably in this section, and they mean the same thing. Similarly, destructive, inappropriate, and unhealthy expressions of anger will be used likewise.

We should always strive to have positive relationships with our spouses. That means we should not get angry at every little thing. Let us look at the mathematical expression of anger to illustrate our point. You married your spouse for better or for worse. He or she is part of your everyday life. If you get angry at any little thing, can you imagine how many times you are going to be angry in a day or in a week? Let us assume that you get angry at little things every other day. That translates to being angry an average of three times in a week. Mathematically, that means angry episodes twelve times a month for minor things. In a year, you will have had 144 angry episodes.

A spouse who gets angry over little things has the potential to have major angry episodes. Let us assume this particular spouse has two major angry episodes in a month. That adds up to twenty-four major angry episodes in a year. Can you imagine being in a marriage where your spouse has that many angry episodes in a year—or even half of it? The point here is that if we think of the many times we could have gotten angry, or even were angry, it may dawn on us how important appropriate management or appropriate expressions of anger are in marriage.

A spouse who knows how to express his or her anger appropriately can distinguish between which precipitating issues warrant an angry response and which do not. In marriage, we are faced with such situations every day, and this is where our anger expressive skills come into play. In the best interest of our marriages, and for our own mental and physical well-being, it is not good to get angry at every little thing. It is pertinent to ignore some minor infractions in marriage. We have to be selective about what is important to address and what needs to be left alone. This is necessary because sometimes certain things not properly addressed can result in big issues. As the dust settles

LOVE AND MARRIAGE PERSPECTIVES

or emotions calm down, we may even realize that some things were not a big deal after all. In marriage, we should be careful not to make mountains out of molehills.

Constructively, anger can be used to solve problems in marriage. It can further be used to hurt your spouse if expressed destructively. Destructive anger can result in belittling your spouse, either by overt or covert hostility. When it is all over, we end up regretting our actions and wishing we'd never expressed our anger destructively. However, the harm is already done, and no amount of regret can take our actions back. Our spouses may forgive, but they may never forget. Healthy expressions of anger, on the other hand, bring clarity, whereby both spouses express their concerns and address issues relating from what was expressed. Boundaries are set and expectations defined. The most constructive expression of anger in marriage is when you use the outcome of that anger to promote understanding between you and your spouse. You can vent, but do not let that lead to control or demanding submission from your spouse. An outcome from anger that results in intimidating our spouses or leads to an outcome that the marriage is worse off prior to the anger is destructive in that it affects the marriage adversely. An appropriate or constructive expression of anger is an outcome that either advances the marriage or fosters an understanding without regressing the marriage. Healthy expressions of anger should be balanced so both spouses see the outcome as a win-win situation and the marriage floats along healthy.

ANGER IN MARRIAGE

In marriage, a spouse can get angry, but it should not be too often. When that spouse gets angry, he or she should not let that anger last too long. In expressing that anger, consider your marriage and be sure not to do things that will hurt the stability of your marriage.

When anger takes control

Do not let anger take control of you or your marriage. Your spouse may react negatively when you act like a different person altogether. Let us assume that the husband is the one who gets angry. When anger takes control, the husband loses rational thought. The wife may want to go through therapy as a condition of continued marriage. He may get angry about that stipulated condition by his wife—or even deny that he needs any help. Sometimes the husband may start blaming the wife for precipitating his anger. When responsibility is not accepted by the husband and blame is projected to the wife, that anger has gotten out of hand and out of control.

Because of the anger, the marriage faces increased frustration and resultant hostility throughout the environment and household. There is the likelihood that either one or both spouses could start lashing out at each other at this stage. The husband could be lashing out because of his inability to control his anger. The wife could be lashing out because she is frustrated with her husband not getting help and having angry episodes most of the time. By this point, she may not care about the marriage anymore and may start resisting the husband's authority.

The marriage will begin deteriorating and will no longer be fulfilling. This can lead to an affair by one or even both spouses, for there is no more loyalty due to the marriage being paralyzed by anger. The marriage is no longer functioning as it should due to affairs, lack of loyalty, anger, stagnation, and no leadership. The sad situation of the marriage leads to more anger and more dysfunction, and it is just a matter of time before the marriage collapses completely. That is a typical example of how destructive anger can be, even contributing to the demise of a marriage.

When to let anger go

The letting-go process is when enough is enough and it's time to ditch your anger and move on with your life. It's healthy to determine when your anger has served its useful purpose and to let it go. The general rule is that once your feelings are communicated to your spouse, it is time to let go. Beyond this point, anger becomes destructive. Your continued expression of your anger can result in resistance, in which your anger becomes counterproductive.

Remember that anger is a signal that something is wrong in the marriage. When that happens, it is imperative that a couple explore the issue that triggered the anger in the marriage. Once that issue is discovered, the spouses should sit down and try to resolve the issue. When both spouses feel that they have done so satisfactorily, the anger should be let go at that point. Continued expression of anger becomes unhealthy and destructive. Most marriages can be salvaged when spouses learn at what point to let go of their anger.

Anger versus rage

The way we express our anger at any given point in time determines the direction of that danger. By direction, I mean whether it is going to be a negative or positive expression. When we decide to express our anger in a negative, unhealthy, or aggressive way, it can sometimes lead to rage. I used the phrase "decide to express" because it is up to us to channel our anger in the direction that we want it. Channeling in the right direction takes a skill known as appropriate anger management. In discussing the difference between anger and rage, one should take into account that anger is a strong expression of emotion. Rage is more powerful and more volatile than anger. Rage is the severest of angry emotions. Technically, it is anger out of control, which leads first to hostility and then to rage. If we can measure anger by an infusion of adrenaline into our bodies, and we then assume that anger is one jolt or dose of adrenaline, then rage is a triple or quadruple dose of adrenaline. Rage is therefore the extreme expression of human emotion. It can also be stated that anger, if out of control, can result in hostility, and unchecked hostility leads to rage. So rage is anger plus hostility run amuck.

> *Make no friendship with an angry man, and with furious man do not go, lest you learn his ways and set a snare for your soul.* (Proverbs 22:24–25)

Biblical expressions of anger

The first mention of anger in the Bible is in Genesis (4:5), where it states that Cain was angry. Cain did not manage his anger appropriately. His anger was severe in that he killed his brother Abel.

Another Biblical mention of anger is Saul's anger against Jonathan. It shows how anger can drive somebody to rage. This was recorded in I Samuel 20:30–34:

> *Then Saul's anger was aroused against Jonathan, and he said to him, "You son of a perverse, rebellious woman! Do I not know that you have chosen the son of Jesse to your own shame and to the shame of your mother's nakedness? For as long as the son of Jesse lives on the earth, you shall not be established, nor your kingdom. Now therefore, send and bring him to me, for he shall surely die. And Jonathan answered Saul his father, and said to him, "Why should he be killed? What has he done?" Then Saul cast a spear at him to kill him, by which Jonathan knew that it was determined by his father to kill David. So Jonathan arose from the table in fierce anger, and ate no food the second day of the month, for he was grieved for David, because his father had treated him shamefully.*

Note the strong words as he talked about his mother's nakedness. This is rage in action. You can see from the above that:

An angry man stirs up strife, and a furious man abounds in transgression. (Proverbs 29:22)

The first mention of anger in the Bible is in Genesis 4:5. I have addressed the circumstances surrounding that above. The last mention of dealing with anger in the Bible is in Revelation. Another interesting correlation is already emerging, for Genesis is the first book of the Bible, and Revelation is the last book, or writing, in the Bible, and anger was mentioned both in the beginning and in the end. The last is from Revelation 19:15:

Now out of His mouth goes a sharp sword, that with it He should strike the nations. And He Himself will rule them with a rod of iron. He Himself treads the winepress of the fierceness and wrath of Almighty God. And he has on His robe and on His thigh a name written: KING OF KINGS AND LORD OF LORDS.

God is compassionate, not angry

As Christian husbands and wives, we need to understand how the emotion of anger works. This will help us in our relationships with our spouses and with God. The first issue that needs to be addressed is the erroneous notion that anger is sin, that if we get angry, we are sinning against God. Anger is an emotion. It is the way that we express that emotion that matters. Sometimes people tend to confuse anger with hate.

In several instances in the Old Testament, it was reported that God was angry, prompting some people to conclude that God is an angry God. In most instances, it was with the people of Israel for the rebellion, transgressions, idolatry, and worship of other false Gods. The Israelites of that time flagrantly violated almost every tenet and covenant that God gave them, and naturally, he expressed his anger at them. The key to this expression was that it was intended to correct them because he did not want to forsake them. Proverbs 3:11–12 says this about correction:

My son, do not despise the chastening of the LORD, nor detest His correction; for whom the Lord loves He corrects.

I previously mentioned confusing anger with hate. God's anger is meant to correct, not to punish. His anger is love, not hate. God's anger was expressed out of love to correct and remedy a broken relationship. If one follows the scripture carefully and analyzes the implication, the intention of that writing will be clear. So God's intention regarding his use of anger is love, correction, and as a good shepherd, keeping the flocks together. Anger brings seriousness to relationships. It also brings clarity and reality to the relationship if expressed appropriately. We may want to be careful about the way we teach anger in Sunday schools or in preaching the Gospel. We should discard any teaching linking God as angry and punitive. We should teach that his anger is to show love and correct people who are not following his commandments. God is a compassionate and merciful God. Instances of his compassion and mercy abound in the Bible.

Is anger sinful?

Let us explore the notion that anger is sinful. Anger is not sinful. Anger is a complex emotion. God is above sin. He cannot sin. Obviously, his expression of anger is not sinful. If you as a husband tell your wife, "Honey, I am angry at you," does that mean that you committed a sin? Obviously not; what you did was communicate your feelings, which included anger, and then expressed that anger. Your wife may want to explore the issue that made you angry, and you can work that out together. When it is worked out, the circumstance necessitating your anger is corrected and the relationship moves on smoothly. It is important to reiterate that the way the anger is expressed is the problem. The Apostle Paul helped debunk the misunderstanding about anger being a sin. In Ephesians 4:26, it is illustrated as follows:

Be angry, and do not sin. Do not let the sun go down on your wrath.

Genesis tells us that we are made in the image of God. We have noticed that God has emotions. Since we are made in his image, it follows that we have emotions also. Expression of anger is a choice. I have previously argued that in this chapter. Our choice of that expression, if it is healthy expression, affects our marriages in a positive light. If we choose an unhealthy or destructive expression of anger, then it affects our marriages negatively.

Do men and women express anger differently?

Men and women get angry. As we have seen at the beginning of this chapter, the way anger is expressed determines the direction of that anger. Some argue that men and women express anger differently, saying that men tend to verbalize more and women bottle their emotions inside. Let us review some of the ways men and women express anger.

Anger expression in men and women

It has been suggested that since God created men and women differently, they respond to issues differently. That reminds me of a book that discussed men and women coming from different planets. When it comes to anger and the way we express it, psychological, cultural, and societal expectations come into play. Men are expected not to cry, not to express feelings through crying. Women tend to express feelings by crying more than men do. When it comes to aggressiveness, men tend to be more aggressive than women are. This is illustrated by men playing more aggressive sports like football, hockey, polo, boxing, wrestling, and other contact sports. Women lag behind in these areas and are less aggressive, perhaps based on their constitutional makeup. A girl who starts developing interest in contact sports may be termed a tomboy.

ANGER IN MARRIAGE

Men are expected to be in control or to take charge in a relationship or marriage. One may argue, however, that in quite a few marriages, females have taken charge. Women are known to be nurturers, peacemakers, and soothers. Men tend to express anger more by verbalizing, while women tend to be more quiet or silent. Sometimes women have a different way of communicating than men do. This includes body language, tone, and voice. When it comes to expression of anger, all the above-mentioned factors play a part between a man and woman—and a husband and wife, for that matter. Further, I want to add that no criterion dictates specifically how a wife or husband reacts to anger in marriage. The harmony or disharmony in a marriage most of the time dictates one's reaction to anger. The personality of the wife or husband also comes into play. Having stated that, let us now explore anger in marriage.

Marital anger

Marriage is the coming together of two personalities. Remember that those two personalities also include two different sets of emotions. Despite being one flesh, those differing personalities and emotions are complex and complicated insofar as how they express themselves. Marriage is about emotions, which is why marriage, in most instances, generates more anger than any other relationship. Remember that anger is also about emotions. Anger is good in marriage if expressed appropriately because it helps couples communicate their feelings toward each other. What is bad about anger in marriage is when it is expressed destructively. This is why it is good for a couple to learn how to react to anger in the course of their marriage. Yes, an anger plan is good for marriage, in that anger is unavoidable in marriage, and your plan is what keeps your relationship going smoothly.

Nonverbal communication as an expression of anger in marriage sends a wrong message, for there is no clarity of communication in nonverbal messages. Can you imagine what the reaction of your spouse would be at even the slightest expression of anger if you glare, flash, or roll your eyes, in that it can be interpreted in any way? On the surface, it mostly signals that you do not care. Factor in other issues like personalities, emotions, issues that precipitated the anger, and the state of the marriage, and that expression can mean anything. The point here is that in marital expression of anger, do not do anything that will escalate the anger. Consider the scenario that we were discussing above. If you raise your voice while responding to his or her expression of anger, do you think that it will escalate or de-escalate the anger? It will definitely escalate the anger. In Proverbs, it is stated:

A soft answer turns away wrath, but a harsh word stirs up anger. (Proverbs 15:1)

Following the same scenario we were discussing, what if the spouse responding to that expression of anger slammed the door or slapped his or her spouse? You probably guessed it; things would fall apart. That brings us to our first rule about anger in marriage.

Rule #1: Never respond to anger with anything that may aggravate or escalate the situation. It does not matter who or what precipitated the anger. That will be examined at the exploratory stage. At this stage, the key is to de-escalate the anger.

Acknowledging anger in marriage

Anger is a necessary occurrence in marriage. Remember that anger is communication, and communication is necessary for marriage to function. The way you manage anger in marriage can determine whether the marriage will survive. Anger is a death knell in marriage only if the spouses in the marriage make it that way. They can do so by not having a plan or by lacking the necessary skills to respond to anger. Accept that you are angry, and if you are the cause of the anger, find ways to resolve it by taking the lead. It does not matter who leads or has control in the family. If the wife is the one in the wrong, she should initiate the lead, and vice versa. If the spouse responsible for that anger asks for forgiveness, is it appropriate for the other spouse to remain angry? No. It sounds easy in theory, but in practice, the spouse should learn to forgive.

Rule #2: Acknowledge anger. If you are the cause of the anger, accept it. Do not rationalize or justify it. Forgive your spouse in the same way Christ forgave you. The next time around, it could be you who precipitates the anger and needs to ask for forgiveness.

LOVE AND MARRIAGE PERSPECTIVES

Sex and Anger in Marriage

Some couples withhold sex when they are angry as a way to punish, get even, or express anger. If so, do not be surprised during one of those special moments when you touch your spouse and his or her response is, "Don't touch me. I'm angry at you." If you are like me, that will kill all desire for sex. That may not be a good time to try to resolve the issue, unless it is something that can truly be resolved quickly. You do not want to give your spouse the impression that you want to resolve the issue quickly just to get to the sex. Sex is for the spouses to enjoy each other, and withholding sex because one spouse is angry is not quite what sex is intended for in marriage. However, one will argue that sex is emotion and anger is emotion as well. So is sex appropriate when one spouse is not emotionally ready for sex? I think the way it is communicated and the way that communication is received is what counts, but this is a gray area. It is better for the couples concerned to decide that, depending on what their anger plans say about the issue. You may be realizing now why anger plans makes sense in marriage.

Sex, on the other hand, can be used as a way to make up after the resolution of an angry episode. The danger here is not resolving an issue and then rushing to have sex. In that instance, sex is being used as an appeasement. The sex may be good, but the issue remains unsolved. In your mind, you may be feeling good, but probably not if the issue hasn't been resolved. The only way to resolve an issue is to talk about it. As for anger, you talk about it and explore alternatives as to how to prevent the same issue from recurring.

Rule #3: Do not withhold sex as a punishment, to get even with your spouse, or as a way to express anger. However, do not use sex as a way to appease your spouse, thinking the issue will be resolved once you have had sex.

Marital anger due to imbalance

This probably needs some explanation for clarity. Imbalance here refers to imbalance of power. One spouse is afraid the other spouse has more power in the marriage. The spouse that is perceived to have more power makes major decisions about money management, initiation of sex, communication, buying a new car, where to live, and so on. It is essentially about control—who control things in the marriage. This is another reason to have a plan in the marriage. Issues like this are exhaustively discussed, about who does what in the marriage. This is the good old power struggle, which further leads to the issue of submission in marriage.

I stated in the chapter about the husband and wife that submission is not automatic. It is contingent on the husband loving the wife, and the more the husband loves the wife, the more the wife submits to the husband. The issue of power struggle and control should not be an issue in a healthy marriage. Power, control, and submission fall under division of labor, where husband or wife is assigned a specific task. With this assignment, each controls or makes a decision about what is assigned to him or her. A healthy balance is therefore maintained, and this type of anger is reduced to the barest minimum. The way to maintain or achieve this balance is through negotiation. The outcome of that negotiation is then entered into the marriage plan. If an angry episode happens because of that and it is resolved, the resolution is entered on the anger plan. I further argued in my chapter on submission that submission is mutual. When husband and wife submit to each other, there are fewer problems. Ephesians 5:21 consists of one sentence, and it says it all:

Submitting to one another in the fear of God.

That is the balance I am talking about in marriage.

Rule #4: Share power and do not let one spouse have all control in the marriage. The exception is if one spouse declines it. Strike a balance in your marriage and let submission be mutual and reciprocal.

Communicating anger in marriage

The way you perceive angry feelings in marriage may correspond to the way your spouse reacts to them. Communicating anger is necessary to let your spouse know how you feel, but the way you communicate it is vital. Do not be like Adam, who started blaming Eve for giving him the forbidden fruit. In communicating anger, do not use the "you" word; instead, use the "I" word to express your anger. For example, never tell your spouse this: "*You* made me angry because ..." Instead, say this: "I was angry because ..." When you use the "you" word, you are already blaming and passing judgment. In anger and in behavior, the only person or behavior you can control is yours. It does not matter who caused whom to be angry. Control yourself, your behavior, and your anger. Your spouse is responsible for controlling his or hers. When both of you have controlled yourselves and things have calmed down, you can sit down and discuss the issue together.

Rule #5: Do not blame your spouse. Blaming may make the issue of anger more difficult to resolve. A verbal attack is the same as being judgmental, and it shows that you are not ready to resolve the issue. A physical attack connotes anger and probably rage. You have just escalated the situation instead of de-escalating it.

Husband/wife anger releasing technique

One technique for a husband and wife to use to manage their anger is anger releasing or venting sessions, also known as anger defusing sessions. The objective of this is for couples to get together and air out their grievances. This is beneficial in marriage because it helps both spouses discuss how they feel about issues in the marriage. As these issues are discussed, spouses take a mental note of what made the other spouse angry and explore the issues in detail. Clarifications are noted and alternatives explored. How to react in a similar situation is explored and noted on the anger plan. How to prevent the same issue or incident from recurring is also noted. This fosters communication and understanding between couples. Remember that marriage is about communication and fostering peace and harmony. These types of sessions are like killing two birds with one stone because they achieve the objectives of communication and peaceful coexistence. There is a strong correlation between venting and longevity in marriage, for when couples get together to address issues, there is the likelihood that they will have fewer problems compared to couples that do not address their marital issues.

It would be beneficial to approach these sessions with seriousness, as one would a business meeting—not necessarily in suit and tie, but the manners, speech, and comments should be cordial. Both husband and wife should respect each other at the sessions. There should be no cursing or foul language. Stick to issues at hand; do not go back to issues already discussed unless it is agreed that they are part of the agenda. It may also be necessary to agree in advance on the issues to be discussed, perhaps writing them down on a piece of paper prior to the session. Remember that what you want is for your marriage to run smoothly. These types of sessions offer you that chance, so do not blow the opportunity to resolve the angry situation.

Rule #6: Remember that it is beneficial to have some type of procedure for you and your spouse to air your grievances. These types of sessions enhance understanding in marriage. As love between you and your spouse increases due to clarity from the sessions, vitality is injected into your marriage.

Do not sweat the small stuff

In marriage, it may be pertinent to overlook certain things. Couples should try not to get angry at every little thing. You are in a marriage to complement and enjoy each other. By no means am I advocating that you not air or vent any angry situation. Similarly, avoid crying wolf when there is no wolf. Both spouses should find alternatives to anger and be slow to anger, as mentioned in Proverbs 19:11:

> *The discretion of a man makes him slow to anger, and his glory is to overlook a transgression.*

Rule #7: Do not sweat the small stuff in marriage.

Some questions to consider

In some chapters in this book, I discussed strategies to consider. Now I'm going to list some questions to consider. The reason for this is that in anger, the more the individual probes himself or herself, the more that person has insight into the anger. Consider the following:

LOVE AND MARRIAGE PERSPECTIVES

(1) Where is my anger coming from? Could it be the way that I relate to my wife or my husband? What is the origin of my anger?

(2) Why should I let my anger control me? Shouldn't I be the one controlling my anger?

(3) Why should I let my anger affect my wife or my husband? Is my anger letting me be the loving husband or wife that I am supposed to be?

(4) Are these angry feelings letting me to be a good role model for my husband or wife? Am I being a positive influence on my children?

(5) Why should I let my anger get the better part of me?

(6) If my wife or husband refuses to have sex with me, am I not making my marriage worse by throwing temper tantrums?

(7) Isn't it more appropriate to explore with my wife or husband the reason for denying me sex? Wouldn't that be a better alternative, helping to resolve the issue? If these issues are resolved, won't I have a better understanding of my husband or wife? Won't resolution of the problem give me a better chance of getting sex next time around?

(8) What efforts am I making to prevent the situation that made me angry from recurring? If I am faced with the same situation,

how will I behave toward my wife or husband?

(9) Do I want my wife or husband to divorce me? Won't my repeated angry episodes lead to divorce?

(10) What type of help should I get to help me work on angry feelings? Should I get counseling through a licensed professional or go to my pastor for pastoral counseling?

If you look at these questions carefully, you will see that they are focused on "I" questions, not "you" or "we." When you ask the "I" questions, you focus on yourself. In behavior and anger, the only person you can control is yourself. You are responsible for your own behavior and should avoid projecting blame to your spouse. Answering these questions honestly will probably help you understand your anger by giving you insight into it. With this insight and knowledge after this self-analysis and assessment, the process for getting help for your anger should begin. Anger can make a marriage. It can also break or unmake a marriage. That choice is entirely yours.

Conclusion

In concluding this chapter, it is important to state that anger is an emotion. It is best to discover the emotions underneath your anger. Once you are able to do so, you can begin the process of managing your anger. It should be reiterated about the imperativeness of anger management in marriage. Anger impacts your marriage negatively or positively, depending on your management style. We should never let our anger progress to aggression in marriage. A key element is to know at what point to interrupt your anger on the continuum scale of anger, from hostility to aggression. Again, anger is an emotion. Hostility is an attitude, and aggression is the resultant behavior meant to harm the person the anger is directed toward. Your spouse may keep a distance from you if you become aggressive or hurtful. Other people may avoid you, rejecting you because of your aggressive episodes. There is also guilt and shame that you have to deal with when you calm down and realize how your actions have affected your spouse. Your wife or husband may not be physically close to you for days or even weeks, depending on how severely he or she is impacted by your anger. With each angry episode, your marriage regresses instead of progresses. Depending on the continuity and frequency of your angry episodes, your marriage may never recover, and your spouse may be consulting a divorce attorney.

Your anger could be a signal that some of your needs are not being met in the marriage. Depending on what makes you angry, it could also mean that you are not addressing an important emotional issue in your life or in the marriage. Anger is a direct emotion if you understand your anger. It can be a tricky emotion if you do not understand your anger. Your anger could be a warning that two or three other things are happening, perhaps that you are giving too much or compromising your values too much. It could further mean that you are compromising too much of your beliefs in the relationship. On the other hand, it could also mean that you are giving too little in the marriage, causing your anger to become misdirected. That is the tricky nature of anger. So your management or expressive style or pattern is everything in anger, in turn impacting your marriage.

For every minute you are angry you lose sixty seconds of happiness.

—Ralph Waldo Emerson

CHAPTER TWELVE
Attitude in Marriage

Whenever you're in a conflict with someone, there is one factor that can make the difference between damaging your relationship and deepening it. That factor is attitude.
—William James

THE MOMENT THEY say "I do," many people fantasize about living happily ever after in their marriages. Most matrimonial vows incorporate Utopian views in which couples pledge their love forever. This fantasy of happiness makes couples pledge for better or for worse, until death do them part. Do not get me wrong—I believe in marriages and in those pledges. The realization of it all depends largely on our attitude, which is a deal maker in marriage. Attitude is also a deal breaker. The types of attitudes that we exhibit in our marriages determine how happy or unhappy our marriages will be. This reminds me of an adage: "As you make your bed, so you must lie on it." It is the same with attitude. We are our own attitudes, for the types of attitudes that we project define us. With his attitude, a person can make his marriage a bed of roses. In the same way, his attitude can also make it a pain in the rear end. I have seen people debate about attitude. Some argue that attitude is everything. Others take the approach that attitude is being overblown and is not all that is purported to be. I have always believed in an eclectic approach to issues. My take on it is that in marriage, multiple factors, as opposed to singular factors, influence outcome. However, our attitudes largely influence marital outcome. Is attitude innate, learned, or developed? It is appropriate to review it at this point.

Predisposition of attitude

There is always this question about attitude, whether it is predisposed or developed. Attitude is developed, although I prefer to use the word learned. Attitude is a learned behavior. Everything about attitude is good. Why? The answer is simple. If the attitude that you learned is good, you keep that attitude. If, on the other hand, you learned a bad attitude, you let go of the bad attitude. So attitude is learned and unlearned. It is, however, important to let go of the bad attitude. Sometimes the type of reward or satisfaction we get from an attitude can make us keep a bad attitude while knowing full well that the behavior itself is bad. A typical example is drug use. We know that drugs are addictive. They affect our lives negatively, yet we refuse to let go of that bad attitude of using drugs because of the high or false sense of euphoria that we get from doing drugs. We are really our own attitude in that we choose which type of attitude we tend to project or exhibit. Yes, attitude is a choice. It is up to us to make the right choice regarding attitude because it affects our marriages.

Attitude as a choice

As stated above, attitude is a choice. If someone makes a positive choice, he has a positive attitude, which leads to a positive marriage. If he makes a negative choice, it results in a negative attitude, which affects marriage negatively. Let us illustrate this with an example. Let us imagine that I got married, and within six months, I started having an affair with my ex-girlfriend. Let us further imagine that my marriage was going fine. My spouse is dedicated to the marriage and does her best to live according to the dictates of her marriage vow. I am fully aware of the impact an affair has on a marital relationship, yet I chose to continue with the affair until I got caught. I had the choice to abide by my marriage vows, but I did not. I had the choice not to associate with my ex-girlfriend, but I exercised that choice negatively, and my attitude affected my marriage negatively. I also had the choice not to have extramarital affairs, but I chose the attitude that devastated my spouse and my marriage. This is an example of how our attitudes can influence our marriages negatively or positively. The result of that effect is individual. We should accept responsibility for our behaviors and attitudes and not blame our spouses for bad choices.

My wife forgives me—what happens now?

If my wife forgives in the above scenario, I should count myself lucky and should not go back to the same behavior. We talked about attitude being a learned behavior. The same way that I learned to be unfaithful to my wife is the way I will learn being faithful to her. My wife's attitude, which is to forgive me, is her choice. She exercised an attitude of forgiveness—making a choice to forgive. Her attitude impacted our marriage positively, for the marriage continued. If she had chosen an unforgiving attitude, which is also her choice, the marriage would have been affected adversely. She made a choice after a careful review of what was best for her and the marriage under the circumstances. The best thing for me is always to have an attitude of repentance and spirit of contrition, for forgiveness is not forgetfulness. My attitude of repentance will make my wife not to remember my unfaithfulness until there is a recurrence. How can we avoid repeating our bad attitudes in marriage? Let us review that issue.

Recurrent bad attitude

A bad attitude affects our marriages negatively; a recurrent bad attitude affects our marriages adversely. To avoid recurrence, three basic things need to happen. First, we do a self-assessment. Second, we devise a plan based on the outcome of the assessment. Third, we set up a mechanism to implement our plan. This is also known as the action stage. Let us review each stage and see how it impacts our attitude and marriage.

Assessment

We know our inner selves better than anyone else does. There are, however, things about us that we do not know. This is

ATTITUDE IN MARRIAGE

because the way we perceive ourselves could be different from the way that others perceive us. Since we are talking about attitudes in marriages, it is imperative that we solicit the help of our spouses to help us in our self-assessments. There may be certain things about our attitudes that are bothering our spouses, and we can include them in our self-assessments. In doing this assessment, be honest with yourself and bring up issues that will help your marriage so you can work on them. There is nobody that I can think of who does not have issues or attitudes to work on in marriage. Even if you think that you do not have any issues to work on, at least you can improve on the good attitude that you already have. As far as this world is concerned, there is always room for improvement. Thinking that we do not need any improvement in our lives is a denial and avoidance of reality.

In this self-analysis, or assessment, our questions will help us probe issues within ourselves. This probing will reveal to us who we are. Sometimes we think that we know ourselves, but that is not always the case. A hypothetical example would be what led me to be unfaithful to my wife when we discussed attitude as a choice. What made me choose to have an affair with my ex-girlfriend? Am I not getting enough sex from my wife? If I am not getting enough sex from my wife, how can I resolve that with my wife? If I do not resolve that with my wife, will I be unfaithful again? Is there a particular type of sex that my ex-girlfriend gives me that my wife is not giving me? Assuming that is the situation and this tripe of sex is not deviant or perverted, how can I get my wife to give me this type of sex? Let us further assume that my affair with my ex-girlfriend is perverted and deviant. How can I stop having this type of sex? Do I need professional counseling to avoid or stop this type of sexual behavior? What impact will this type of sex act have on my marital and professional life? What type of behavior or attitude am I exhibiting to my wife with my sexual acts and attitudes? If we have children, how will they perceive me if they know about this attitude? The reason I am including a variety of questions on just one issue is to illustrate how in-depth probing can reveal the intended outcome that will help a person change or adjust his attitude. The above questions are illustrative only, and in no way suggest that sexual issues are the only attitudes that we need to adjust in our marriage.

Sexual issues manifested due to my affair with my ex-girlfriend. There may be other issues like anger, lack of respect, money management, housework, excessive drinking, and other unmanifested issues that we need to probe. Remember that the objective in most marriages is to live happily ever after, so we need to incorporate in our assessment things that will make the marriage stress-free. The more things we include in our assessment, the better the outcome. Note that just because you may have multiple things in your self-assessment does not indicate that you are a bad person. Attitude is not a person. It is a behavior. In the same way that you learned something, you can unlearn it. The fact of your including all the relevant factors means that you are honest, realistic, love your spouse, and are anxious to have a happy, stress-free marriage.

Plan

This stage is when you translate your findings from the assessment into a workable plan. You can even write down your plans. You might have noticed that I used the word "workable" to qualify the plan. That means your plan should not be ambiguous. The plan should be realistic, achievable, and implementable. It should also have a time frame. Note that this plan is not written in stone once it is made. It is always subject to review. This review is needed as other behaviors are manifested. You can further evaluate or review your plan even in the absence of any behavior manifesting. Over time, you can come up with a better plan that suits the attitude that you are trying to adjust or address. A typical plan can look like this, or it may incorporate those elements stated above.

(a) If I think of being unfaithful, I will channel that thought to how much I love my wife, and how she forgave me when she caught me cheating. I will consistently resist any urge to cheat on my wife. If that urge persists, I will call my wife and tell her how much I love her—and what she and my marriage means to me. This will help distract me and displace that urge.

(b) When I am angry, I will not overreact. I will go to another room and calm down. After I calm down, I will discuss with my wife the reason for my anger. When she is giving me her feedback, I will not interrupt her and will respect her feelings and opinions, encouraging her to talk out. If I am wrong or precipitated the incident, I will accept responsibility for my behavior and not blame my wife.

(C) I will not deprive my wife of sex if she initiates it or asks for it. I will not use sex as a punishment for what she did wrong. Withholding sex from her under these circumstances would inject another stress into our marriage. I should be more concerned with de-escalating problems in my marriage rather than escalating them.

Again, the above are examples. There is no way of stating what constitutes a perfect plan. Whatever plan you write, as long as it takes stress away from your marriage, addresses the attitude in question, meets the criteria of not being ambiguous, and is implementable and achievable, it translates as a good plan. You will notice in the three given examples that the word "I" is used consistently. There is no use of "you," "we," or "us." This is meant to focus your behavior on yourself. Talking about your spouse's culpability removes the focus from your own behavior. Remember that you are responsible for your own behavior and your own attitude. It would also be a good idea to include your spouse when writing this plan. The rationale for that is that he or she was part of the assessment, and the outcome of the assessment that she was part of is what is being addressed in the plan. His or her input becomes imperative for effective resolution.

Action or implementation

The implementation stage is where the rubber meets the road. This is also where all the talking stops and the action begins. If you are serious about changing your attitude, show it at this stage. If you are serious about caring for your marriage and taking it to the next level, this is your time to show it. I call this stage "show time" because it is time to show your attitude. It can also be termed the "put-up or shut-up" stage. The reason is that if you have this nice plan written and cannot even do most of the things on it, what good is your plan?

Back to the scenario of cheating on my wife within six months of marriage, if she forgave me, even helping me do my assessment and the writing of my plans, yet I continue cheating on her with my ex-girlfriend, despite her help and forgiveness. What type of attitude am I still projecting? To earn her forgiveness, I'd promised her that I would no longer be unfaithful. Does it mean that I wasted her time by letting her believe that I would no longer cheat with my ex-girlfriend? Did I take her for granted when I started doing the very thing that I promised her I would not do? Am I not stupid for continuing to exhibit that type of attitude? Why even call this woman an ex-girlfriend if it is obvious that I continue to associate with her and have sex with her? Why am I having sex outside my marriage instead of following God's plan? Who would blame my wife if she decides to divorce me for repeated unfaithfulness?

The reason for exploring these issues is to illustrate that your plan is not worth the paper that it is written on if you do not implement it according to the plan. Take into account that the purpose of that plan was to change my attitude and advance the marriage. By not following the plan, not only did I not change my attitude, but also I regressed my marriage. This is another example of how our attitudes affect our marriages. The type of attitude one exhibits in marriage can help or hurt a marriage. Attitude precipitates stress in marriage. The more positive the attitude, the more the marriage moves in a positive direction, and vice versa. It is up to each of us to decide which direction we want our marriage to go. That direction will be a direct result of our attitude.

Causes of bad attitude in marriage

Several factors are responsible for bad -- or negative -- attitudes in marriage. They include but are not limited to stress, unfaithfulness, phobias, anger, resentment, and past experiences. For purposes of this chapter, I will discuss how past experiences can interject negative attitude. I will further discuss how past experiences, if addressed, can enhance marriage. In other chapters on this book, I have addressed some of the factors stated above. Let us review how past experiences, if unaddressed, can impact marriages negatively.

Unresolved past experiences

You would be amazed how a person's past continues to be part of his present when it comes to unresolved issues. In marriage, patience and understanding should supersede irrational thoughts, especially when those thoughts cannot be justified. Let me explain what I mean. Sometimes your spouse's attitude may not be what you think it should be. However, consider this: have you ever bothered to find out why your spouse's attitude has been the way it is? Your spouse may have some unresolved issues that he or she brought into the marriage. Your spouse's attitude may continue the way it is until that issue is resolved. An example will make this clearer. When an associate of mine, let us call him Panda, came back from his honeymoon, he was talking about annulling his marriage. He had been married for only two weeks. I asked Panda why not reconsider—after all, he'd just gotten married, and he should give his marriage a chance. He stated that there was no meaningful sex during the honeymoon, and he did not see how he could live with a woman who didn't cherish sex the way he did. They had not engaged in premarital sex, because his spouse did not believe in sex prior to marriage. They were engaged for over a year, and according to Panda, he thought that their first night should be a blast. It turned out that his wife was raped when she was an adolescent. That incident made her uninterested in sexual relations. Panda's advances reminded her of that rape. The marriage recovered after counseling, and they had a fulfilling marriage after that unresolved issue got resolved.

LOVE AND MARRIAGE PERSPECTIVES

Your response to attitude matters

We have discussed having a plan to help us deal with our attitudes. This plan helps us focus on how to conduct ourselves. This helps us move our marriages in a positive direction. That is why in marriage, the way we *respond* to attitude counts, not the way we *react* to it. When we respond, it should be positive and constructive. When we react, it is emotion-based, and the outcome is usually negative. With an attitude response plan, you are more thoughtful and rational in your response because forethought was involved. With a plan, we are being proactive rather than reactive, better equipping us to deal with it. Responding rather than reacting puts us in control to deal with any manifesting attitude. An example could be your wife cooking and appearing frustrated for whatever reason. If you *respond* with a soft, cool voice and even offer to take over the cooking, you will likely defuse the situation. If, on the other hand, you *react* to her comment, you will escalate the situation.

Positive affirmations

Positive affirmations are important in marriage. Positive affirmations not only motivate our marriages but also improve communication. Our daily use of affirmations enhances positive attitude in the marriage. Can you imagine how your spouse would feel if you said something positive to him or her every day? You will make your spouse feel good. People exhibit positive attitudes when they feel good inside; what they feel inside is what they reflect outward. When given, positive affirmations take control of the thoughts of the receiver of the affirmation. When thought is affected, it influences the emotions, which in turn affects attitude. Is it any surprise that when you say, "Honey, you look so good today," your wife's attitude is bubbly? When you give that type of affirmation to your wife, she accepts it, and her subconscious mind reflects what you told her. Positive affirmation triggers positive feelings, which in turn are exhibited in attitude. It is similar to the labeling theory, where one starts acting out the label he or she is given or assigned. Assume your wife is home feeling somewhat depressed for whatever reason. You return and see her in a depressive state and give her the positive affirmation and encouragement she needs. Her attitude may change from depressive to cheerful because of your affirmation. If, on the other hand, you come home and say, "Here we go again. You're always depressed. If it's not anger one day, it's depression or anxiety another day," what you have just done is complicate her situation. Positive affirmation is reinforcement, and when a behavior is reinforced, one has the potential to repeat that behavior. That is how positive affirmation impacts attitude.

Some points to consider

When it comes to attitude and marriage, it is wise to consider the following points. Such consideration could enhance and help your marriage positively:

LOVE AND MARRIAGE PERSPECTIVES

(1) The attitude that you exhibit in your marriage is critical for the survival or the demise of your marriage.

(2) Always evaluate your attitude to see what impact it has on your relationship.

(3) Be nice to your spouse. When you are nice to him or her, it affects the attitude exhibited. If your spouse is happy, that happiness transfers to you. If your spouse is sad, it affects you negatively.

(4) Incorporate your spouse's feelings into the way that you act in the marriage. The health of your marriage depends on the effort that you put into it.

(5) There is a saying that attitude is everything. There is also a saying that love conquers all. Love combined with positive attitude results in a fantastic marriage.

(6) If you value your marriage, maintain a positive attitude, doing whatever it takes to keep that positive attitude.

(7) Visualize and create a realistic dream that you want in your marriage. Focus and be optimistic, and work toward your dream with the right attitude.

(8) Motivation is the key to a positive attitude. The more motivated you are, the more of a positive attitude you exhibit, and the

more your marriage benefits from that attitude and motivation.

(9) Planning is the key. Have an attitude plan that will help you respond to issues in your marriage instead of reacting to them.

(10) If you get knocked down by any issue in marriage, do not give up. That setback could be a setup for a comeback. So do not be bugged by negative attitude.

(11) Remember that in life, everything has a purpose. There is a purpose for your marriage. With a positive attitude, you can discover this purpose and get to know your spouse better.

(12) Remember that you are responsible for your own attitude in marriage. Accept responsibility for your actions and be open to constructive criticism.

(13) Attitude is reciprocal, a two-way street.

(14) Marriage should be about happiness. Do not let your attitude steal your joy.

Concluding remarks

Marriage is a challenge, but attitude can complicate that challenge. When someone exhibits a negative attitude, he should not blame his spouse for causing his bad attitude. Take into account that attitude is a choice, and we choose to express our feelings

LOVE AND MARRIAGE PERSPECTIVES

either rationally or impulsively. We are the result of our own behaviors. We are also the result of our own attitudes. As individuals, we sometimes tend to demand more from others than we would usually give to or demand of ourselves. Our actions or attitudes can knowingly or unknowingly drive our spouses away. So we should be careful about the type of attitudes that we exhibit. In Proverbs, it is written:

> *It is better to dwell in a corner of a housetop than in a house shared with a contentious woman.* (Proverbs 25:24)

We may sometimes be acting in anger and doing things in the marriage that can forever haunt us, causing us to live with regret. We should always act with forethought and consider the consequences of our actions. Remember this:

> *Whoever digs a pit will fall into it, and he who rolls a stone will have it roll back on him.* (Proverbs 26:27)

If you know of anything that will enhance your happiness and understanding in your marriage, it would be wise to look into it. If, on the other hand, you know what will hurt your marriage, it would be unwise to do that:

> *A prudent man foresees evil and hides himself; the simple pass on and are punished.* (Proverbs 27:12)

I started this conclusion with a sentence dealing with challenge.

ATTITUDE IN MARRIAGE

I will also end with another sentence dealing with challenge. Life presents us with challenges and even throws us curveballs. We should not take a defeatist or victim attitude about what life has done to us. Shouldn't you count yourself lucky to be alive? The point of this is that regardless of the challenge you find yourself up against, it is up to you to tackle that challenge head-on. If you believe that you will succeed, you will succeed. If you believe that you will fail, you will fail. The same thing goes for marriage. The way you handle or project your attitude determines the success or failure of your marriage.

Our attitude toward life determines life's attitude toward us.

—John N. Mitchell

CHAPTER THIRTEEN

Spousal Abuse

Domestic violence causes far more pain than the visible marks of bruises and scars. It is devastating to be abused by someone that you love and think loves you in return. It is estimated that approximately 3 million incidents of domestic violence are reported each year in the United States.
—Dianne Feinstein

MARITAL DOMESTIC ABUSE, also known as domestic violence or spousal abuse, encompasses all ages, races, and socioeconomic and educational levels. Even Christians are not immune to this. In addition to discussing marital domestic abuse, alcohol abuse will also be included because sometimes it is a prelude to marital abuse. Let us discuss what the abuser looks like.

Profile of abuser

In marriage, the abuser is typically a male. There are female abusers, but that percentage is negligible. Therefore, this profile will largely focus on the male abusers. Family background is a contributing factor in who will abuse the wife. A child growing up in a family where the father abuses the mother has a high tendency to abuse his own wife. The reason for that is thinking that what his father is doing, abusing his mother, is the proper way to treat a wife. There is a strong correlation between children who grew up in a household where one parent was abusive and those children going on to later abuse their wives or their own children. There is also a correlation between people lacking appropriate conflict resolution skills and growing up and observing adults in their households resolving conflicts aggressively.

The family is an agent of socialization, and children learn by observation, mimicking and exhibiting behavior modeled to them. As they interact and socialize in their family of origin, they internalize those family values and norms, which in this instance, are abuse and aggression. When they grow up, they start exhibiting their internalized behavior, which is why they have that high propensity to abuse their mate or their children. Spousal abuse affects everybody in the family. Imagine being a child in the home and watching your mother being abused and being powerless to stop it. What do you think that will do to child's self-esteem? It is pertinent at this time to review the types of abuse to give us more insight in this area.

Types of abuse

In spousal abuse, three distinct types are evident: verbal, physical, and emotional. Let us review patterns and characteristics of each.

Verbal abuse

The husband who abuses the wife starts with being verbal. The tone of his voice becomes louder. That is why, as husbands, we should be careful of voice level or tone of conversations with our wives, for it may be misconstrued as verbal abuse. The abusing husband most often shouts at his wife. This shouting is constant. He does it regardless of who is around. It does not matter to him if children or even his in-laws are there. His voice connotes power and absolute authority, and nobody dares question him or his authority. As he gets more comfortable and unchallenged by his actions, this shouting or verbal abuse escalates to emotional abuse. Even when challenged, that somewhat reinforces his behavior, as he perceives himself as being absolutely in charge and in control. Most abusers have self-esteem issues, and even the abused suffers from low self-esteem. The latter are powerless about their predicament.

Emotional abuse

At this stage, the husband as the abuser is getting more comfortable in his actions. The level of the abuse has increased another notch at this stage. He starts being meaner and to some extent gets a kick out of what he is doing. He will start demeaning and deprecating his wife, insulting her as well. He will call his wife names and may even tell her she is no good. Everything the wife does, he criticizes. Even his favorite dish that he used to tell the wife that he liked before the abuse started is no longer good enough for him. The husband throws temper tantrums at this stage, and the tantrums are almost a daily occurrence. He will start threatening the wife with violence and will advise her that the only reason he has not beaten her up is that he loves her.

The wife, out of naiveté, low self-esteem, and probably fear, will perhaps start believing that the husband loves her, and that she'd better be on her best behavior. Remember that the shouting is still there, and it has increased in intensity. The criticism has elevated to a higher degree. The husband demands sex with impunity, and even their favorite sex positions are no longer pleasing to him. At this point, the husband is probably drinking and abusing alcohol or is even an alcoholic. He probably has sexual affairs behind the wife's back, and the wife had better not question him about it. His is almost a reign of terror, and if there is hell on earth, that is where the wife currently is. Finally, the husband may start slamming doors and swinging at her to give her a taste of what will happen to her if she dares question his authority again. Withholding of privileges, assuming that there have been any up to this point, will be routine. She will be constantly blamed for anything and everything that goes wrong in the marriage and family. If his sexual affairs are a persistent phenomenon, he will withhold sex as a punishment to his wife. When he decides to give her sex, it is probably when his girlfriend is not around or because he is drunk.

Physical abuse

This stage is the climax of the abuse. Abuse is progressive. It progresses from verbal to emotional and finally to physical abuse. Each stage is more severe than the previous one. In other words, the higher the stage of the abuse, the severer the type of abuse the wife gets. With time, the husband becomes more comfortable with the abuse because it is now a routine part of his life. The wife suffers more because the longer the abuse continues, the more her situation deteriorates. She is more helpless and even more confused as to the right course of action to take.

At this physical stage, the husband starts assaulting his wife physically, possibly punching her at will. He might even hit her with objects. Knives aren't out of the question, but punching, slapping, and kicking are the preferred modes of assault. Like the verbal and emotional abuse, he does not care who is around and sometimes perceives in his delusional state of mind that it is his right to punch his wife. No wife should let the abuse go this far; she should have sought help prior to this stage or even left for her own safety. Do they ever leave or seek that help? Let us review that situation by discussing the profile of the victim or the abused.

Profile of the victim or the abused

Most of the time, the abused wife has low self-esteem. She probably came from an abusive family, so she has seen at least one member of her family abused, perhaps her own mother or herself. That gives her the false impression that the abuse is probably okay, a normal occurrence in a marriage. It is possible that she came from a low socioeconomic background or simply lacked the fortitude to discuss her situation with someone else early on in the abuse. Educationally, there is a high possibility that she has a low academic background. She is most likely drinking alcohol but likely not to the extent of the husband. Assuming that she was not imbibing alcohol prior to her marriage, she was likely introduced to alcohol by the husband in the good days of the marriage as a way for them to have fun and be merry. It is likely that the abuse may not have started at the time she was introduced to drinking.

At the verbal stage of the abuse, the wife will appear confused, wondering what she did that prompted a change of behavior in her husband. As the abuse escalates to the emotional stage, she becomes an emotional wreck and more confused. She now starts blaming herself, as if the norm, and wants to appease the husband, probably with food and even more sex. The irony with this appeasement is that the more she does it, the more the husband criticizes her and the more empowered he becomes. In this apparent confusion, low self-esteem, and emotional wreckage, some wives even contemplate suicide. If she has a low educational level, she probably will not understand the warning signs or symptoms of her depression as it sets in. She also most likely doesn't have a job and has nobody to discuss her situation with. She cannot leave on her own. The wife becomes completely dependent on the husband.

At the physical stage of the abuse, she will be hiding bruises she got from her husband because of his beatings. Her mode of hiding them could be wearing long sleeves if they are on her arms, or trousers or if they are on her legs. She'll wear makeup if the bruises are on her face. If someone notices her bruises, she also uses denial as a way to cover up the abuse. If you encourage her to leave, she perceives you as intruding in her marriage, and if you are a female, she probably thinks you want her husband as a boyfriend. If there is law enforcement intervention, she is likely to deny the abuse by siding with the husband, and there is a high probability that she will not testify in case she is subpoenaed.

If the husband ever apologizes for the abuse, she will believe that he loves her and have the erroneous impression that he will do better—that the abuse is likely to stop. Probably her parents are divorced, and she will perceive that if she divorces, her life is a failure; she will not want to go through what her parents went through by divorcing. Her marriage is all she has in her mind, and she wants to cling to it at any cost. Assuming that the husband is cheating and she is aware of it, she is unlikely to confront him. She believes that if she remains patient and faithful to her husband, he will love her more, and the abuse will probably subside. She will continue to cling to an unrealistic hope that with time, all these problems will come and pass. Rusbult and Martz (1995) noted: "There is evidence that abused wives who stay with their partners, usually because they perceive poor alternatives, tend to see them as bringing little of value to the relationship."

LOVE AND MARRIAGE PERSPECTIVES

What are the recourse and implications for such a marriage?

The first and obvious recourse in such a marriage is for both spouses to seek professional help, and if the help fails, for the wife to get out of the marriage. This is easier said than done, judging from the profiles of the abuser and the abused. Stating that both should get help assumes some sane thought on the part of the husband to realize what harm he is doing to himself, wife, marriage, children, and family. The chances of the husband realizing that appear remote in some marriages. It is going to take serious prompting and skilled intervention for the wife to leave the marriage for her own safety and that of her children. If she finally summons the courage to leave, there is no guarantee that her delusional husband is not coming after her, probably to settle the score for leaving him. The children are also in a precarious situation regarding their school and where to live. A shelter for abused women may suffice, and what becomes of their fate when the duration of their stay expires at the shelter is even more critical.

She may seek vocational training to acquire the necessary skills for her to compete in the job market. Self-esteem classes to lift her image seem wise. If these things don't happen and her term of residency expires at the shelter, do not be surprised if she ends up with the husband again, as she lacks means of sustenance for her and the children. If she happens to go back to the husband, her rationalization will likely be that the children need their father, and that family should be kept as a unit. That is why in spousal abuse, there are no winners—only losers. Assuming she returns to the husband, there may be a lull in the abuse because the husband received a dose of reality when she left. The abuse will likely return in a matter of days, and the whole pattern will continue. This is why the cycle has to be interrupted, and the only two ways to do so is for one spouse to be away from the other or for both spouses to seek professional help.

Lessons to think about

In marriage, we should love our spouses and not abuse our wives. Since most abusers are male, it is best to be stroking your wife and not striking her. When you show and express love, your marriage flourishes and blossoms. With abuse, you cannot achieve one of the objectives of marriage, which is comfort. In Thessalonians, we were advised as follows:

> *Therefore comfort each other and edify one another, just as you also are doing.* (1 Thessalonians 5:11)

If you are a husband abusing your wife, please get professional help and also think of the legal consequences of your actions. Abuse tends to be perpetual if not interrupted, in that abuse is passed from generation to generation. Remember that children learn abuse as they observe other adults in the household, and they pass some behavior to their own children; hence it's generational. The Bible warned us about generational influences in Exodus:

> *The Lord, the Lord God, merciful and gracious, longsuffering and abounding in goodness and truth, keeping mercy for thousands, forgiving iniquity and transgression and sin, by no means clearing the guilty, visiting the iniquity of fathers upon children and the children's children to the third and the fourth generation.* (Exodus 34:6–7)

As fathers, you do not want to bestow such influence to your children. Be the one who will interrupt that pattern of abuse for the sake of your children. The book of Proverbs advises:

> *Children's children are the crown of old men, and the glory of children is their father.* (Proverbs 17:6)

Alcohol abuse

Alcohol abuse is a serious concern in marriage. When alcohol abuse is combined with spousal abuse, it spells doom for that marriage. It is double trouble for the spouse of the abuser. Following the scenario that men or husbands are the prevalent abusers, let us review how this issue affects marriage. We have reviewed spousal abuse in regard to how it affects marriage. When a husband abuses his wife it follows a pattern. The abuse can happen anytime of the day, night, in that anything can trigger the abuse. In alcohol-related abuse, consumption of alcohol specifically triggers it. Other issues that may have happened while he is drinking could be a secondary factor.

Pattern of abuse

Since he abuses alcohol, the pattern of this abuse is usually in the evenings when he comes home from work and is supposedly relaxing with drinks. When he drinks at those times, it perhaps triggers issues in his mind that the wife did or did not do that are detrimental to the marriage. In his drunken stupor, he senses that the time is ripe to address that issue. In the course of his addressing the issue, he turns violent if things do not go the way he thinks they should. Most abusive husbands have low frustration tolerance, which is why they are abusers in the first place. They lack adequate communication skills and tend to be frustrated with their wives when they fail to get their way or even perceive that they are not getting their way. The resultant effect is striking their wives. Factor the lack of those skills with the entire classic abuse syndrome and compound it with alcohol. What you get is a ticking time bomb ready to explode at any time.

The weekend special

I use the term "weekend special" to refer to a certain type of abuse that occurs mostly on weekends, when the husband is on his usual binge drinking. The timeline of this type of abuse may be between 7:00 p.m. on Fridays and 7:00 p.m. on Sundays. The distinguishing factor in this type of abuse is that it occurs on weekends, and drinking is always involved as a precursor. Suppose that in this example, the husband is paid on Friday, and most of the time, his first place of call after that is the store where he gets his supply of alcohol for the week. He may -- and *may* is the operative word here -- go to the grocery store to buy some food for the family. At this point, his mind is centered on his drinks when he gets home. He does not budget or think of the bills that need to be paid for the week. The rent or mortgage may even be in arrears.

When he gets home, he starts drinking and is jovial with his wife at that point. He is also civil with his children, assuming there are children in the marriage. The cause of his happiness is basically centered on his drinks that he is about to consume. The family will erroneously believe that the happiness is due to his love for his family. In fairness to this type of husband, he loves his family insofar as his own understanding of love, but the mood being discussed here is the euphoria of the alcohol that he is about to consume. As the consumption of the alcohol continues, he begins to lose rational thought. The more he drinks, the more irrational he becomes. Since it is payday, the wife may ask him for money or remind him of that overdue rent—or she may just try to engage him in normal conversation. The husband will then lose all civility. That is when he will tell her what a no-good woman she is. The conflict will escalate from there. If the wife decides to be silent and walk away, the husband takes it as a slight on him. "How dare you walk away when I am talking to you?" If the wife responds in an attempt to deflect his aggression, he also feels slighted. His beef now: "How dare you talk to me that way or even talk when I am talking?" This also results in abuse. The wife is in a no-win situation. The only thing that will save that type of marriage is treatment for his alcohol abuse and life skills management like anger and other abuse-related issues.

Treatment programs

Each state or city provides services on a sliding scale. This allows the client to pay based on his or ability to pay. Those types of programs depend on grants and donations. Most treatment is tailored to fit the individual. A husband who works Monday through Friday can attend the weekend program. The weekend program can either be inpatient or outpatient. Inpatient residential starts on Friday evenings and ends on Sunday evenings. The treatment plan will state the duration of treatment after an intake assessment. Most programs usually last for about ninety days. There are also intensive outpatient programs where the husband can attend seven to twelve hours a day for the duration stated on the treatment plan.

It is not my intention to bore you with the treatment protocol and modalities, but two points must be stated herein. First, the husband must commit and complete treatment or the whole process will be an exercise in futility. Second, he must make a sincere and concerted effort to put into practice all things that he learned at the program and resolve not to assault his wife. Finally, the wife should realize that there is always the danger of relapse. Some treatment programs stipulate a follow-up program in case of relapse.

All marriages are sacred, but not all are safe.
—Rob Jackson

CHAPTER FOURTEEN

Divorce

The only way to stop divorce is to stop marriage.
—Will Rogers

IN DIVORCE, TWO individuals that were a couple decide to begin the process of uncoupling or decoupling their marriage. During the process of uncoupling, the formal initiation, separation, filing of divorce, and ultimately, the finalization of their divorce takes place. These individuals that became one, forming a mutual identity in marriage, end up assuming separate and autonomous identities as the dissolution of their marriage becomes finalized. In the eyes of God, is this a way to resolve marital issues? Are there no other alternatives besides divorce for resolving issues amicably? Does God approve or disapprove of divorce? These and other questions are addressed in subsequent subheadings on this chapter. There are many reasons for couples wanting to divorce, but with the passage of no-fault divorce, any spouse can use the irreconcilable difference clause to file for divorce for any reason. Regardless of the cause of the divorce, children in the marriage are the ones most impacted by the divorce of their parents.

LOVE AND MARRIAGE PERSPECTIVES

Impact of divorce on children

Divorce negatively impacts children more than any other member of the family. This is because their father and mother can move on to other relationships and have some semblance of normalcy in their lives. It should be noted, however, that their subsequent relationships can sometimes further impact their children negatively. This is because a new spouse or cohabitant may in some cases have his or her own issues that result in a disastrous outcome for the children. This outcome can be economic, psychological, social, and emotional. Let us review them.

Economic

Children are impacted economically when their parents' divorce. Divorce disrupts the economic lifeline of children. This is because in divorce in a two-wage earning family where both spouses work, the children most of the time have no choice but to rely mostly on the wage of the custodial parent, usually the mother. In some instances, court-ordered child support payments become difficult to collect. This situation can result in fathers who do not want to pay child support doing all they can to avoid payment. Some fathers quit their jobs or get lower-paying jobs. Either alternative hurts the children because it affects their needed support. When the father gets a lower-paying job, his children get less money in child support. Some fathers do it thinking that they are hurting or getting even with their ex-wives, but the children are the ones most hurt by this action.

Some fathers even move to different states in the quest to avoid child support payments. Can you imagine the devastation when a child goes to bed hungry at the end of the day?

Psychological

Psychologically, children are devastated by the absence of one parent in the household. Children sometimes exhibit anger and conflicting loyalties because of this absence. Sadness and confusion become paramount. The degree of their reaction to those issues depends on the amount of their bitterness. Their ages, the custody arrangements, and the way that they view their parents' marriage are also contributing factors. Some children may result to acting out because of their inability to cope with the divorce. The ability of children to cope with these issues depends on what mechanisms, like after-divorce arrangements, were left by the parents to deal with the acting-out behavior. The more these types of arrangements are made, the better the children are equipped to cope with divorce issues. It is pertinent to add that the children's behavior should be the determining factor in this type of intervention. Professionals in this area, such as licensed clinical social workers, licensed psychologists, licensed professional counselors, and licensed family and marriage therapists, are better-equipped to deal with these issues.

LOVE AND MARRIAGE PERSPECTIVES

Emotional

Can you imagine being a child and feeling sadness that your parents are not living together? Can you further imagine the self-esteem of that child when discussing familial issues at school with children from intact families? This can cause some serious adjustment issues, depending on how that child in particular perceives his parents' divorce. Sometimes complicating these readjustment issues is a remarriage of the custodial parent. When that happens, the new family now becomes a reconstituted family. The children from these reconstituted families have to start getting used to each other, and sometimes their personalities clash because they were raised with different backgrounds and in their eyes and minds, no other substitute or surrogate parent can take the place of the missing parent. Jealousy sometimes manifests because there is a conflict of loyalty not found in traditional, undivorced, intact families. The children have to deal with new mores and folklores in these blended families, thereby resulting in opportunities for disagreements and discord. All these issues further put the children in a precarious situation that spells doom in remarriages and reconstituted families. There is also the issue of instability in remarriages, which may further exacerbate the plight of the children. Chapman (2005, 78) noted: "Sixty percent of those who remarry will experience a second divorce. And if perchance they try it again, the divorce rate for third marriages is seventy-five percent."

This instability is buttressed by the fact that there is a higher divorce rate in remarriages. Chapman's findings are also consistent with the studies of Bumpass and Sweet (1972) and Cherlin (1977). These studies have shown a greater risk of instability and high incidence of divorce for remarriages.

Social

The social trauma is that some children never get to live with the parent of their choice. Children tend to like a particular parent more than the other, and their loyalty is with that parent. Assuming that parent of choice is not the custodial parent, it robs that child of a deep relationship with his father or mother, depending on whom the custodial parent is. Some custodial parents can be vindictive by feeding the children some disinformation about the noncustodial parent, further alienating the children from that parent. The noncustodial father is at a competitive disadvantage then it comes to affection and bonding with the children. Amato (1994) states: "Divorced fathers have become increasingly disadvantaged in terms of emotional bonds with their young adult children when compared to mothers."

Other research further supports how children are negatively impacted by their parents' divorce. Such research includes Amato (1993), McLanahan and Sandefun (1994), and Booth (1999). The above-mentioned research supports the notion that there is a decline in child-parent relations due to the disintegration of the marriage.

If the more affluent parent is not the custodial parent, the children become adversely affected by environmental factors when living in less affluent neighborhoods. The effect of this is the types of schools they attend. Schools in less affluent neighborhoods are less equipped with resources to compete with schools in more affluent neighborhoods. If they end up going to college, the types of colleges that accept them are not high-caliber colleges because of their test scores. The ones lucky enough to be admitted to high-caliber colleges may lack the finances and resources to attend, even with grants. The resultant effect is that the future college education of that child is already precarious, before it even starts, thereby leading to an uncertain quality of life. There is a high likelihood that what happened to their parents' marriage, which included divorce and probably remarriage, may happen to them. Most studies, such as those by Amato (1993) and Cherla (1978), support the above premise.

Stressors in children

Any way you look at it, any divorce-related issues are stressors for the children, whether economical, psychological, emotional, or social. Divorce sets in motion other stressful situations in a child's life, at each stage of the divorce process and beyond. The stress can be in such areas as moving, changing schools, getting situated in a new place, probably moving again, parent remarriage, probably a second divorce, and perhaps a third remarriage. Furstenberg and Nord (1985) noted that: "Children who experienced their parents' divorce are less likely than those from two-biological-parent families to report wanting to be like either mothers or their fathers when they grow up."

This is because with the dissolution of the marriage, children no longer see their parents as role models, and their aspiration takes a dip. In that type of situation, the children need to be encouraged and resocialized to mitigate the failure of their parents. Statistically, the odds stack against children of divorced parents when it comes to having a successful marriage.

Trend and Weeden (2006) noted: "A number of surveys and studies have discovered that adult children of divorce are far more likely to get divorced themselves than are the adult children of intact families (i.e., families in which Mom and Dad did not divorce). Depending on the survey, the child of divorce is at least two to four times more likely to divorce. As if the divorce statistics weren't scary enough, the children of divorce are also more prone to other problems. For instance, they are twice as likely as children from intact homes to drop out of high school. They're twice as likely to become teen parents and unmarried parents. They're also far more likely to become dependent on welfare as adults."

We have already noted how divorce makes children vulnerable to constant episodes of conflict, inadequate parental care, and continued financial hardship. The duration of these stresses depends on the age of the child at the time of the divorce. This is because the stressors continue until the child becomes emancipated, reaches adulthood, or is no longer under the jurisdiction of the family courts. Divorce most often results in severe decline of standard of living for the children and their custodial mothers. This has a stressful impact on the children and a substantial impairment in their overall well-being.

Some points to consider before divorcing

(1) Before you even contemplate divorcing, bear in the mind that God does not like divorce. God does not want us to divorce, for he hates divorce. In fact, in Malachi 2:16, it is stated: "For the Lord God of Israel says that he hates divorce."

(2) As believers and children of God, we love God. Remember what God said: "If you love me, keep my commandments and my will." We keep the commandments of God and his will because we love God. We may not even think of it, but we are going against God's will when we divorce. Why? This is so in that God sanctions Christian marriages. When God approved of marriage between a man and a woman, he even warned that what he has ordained or joined together, let no man put asunder.

(3) Think of the devastating consequences of divorce on your children. They will go through untold hardships during the process of divorce. These hardships continue after divorce. For the children's sake, rethink your position on this issue and remain in your marriage.

DIVORCE

(4) Since we love our children, we should not harm them and should make every attempt to keep them out of harm's way. As we divorce, we harm our own children, thereby acting illogically.

(5) Most divorces are precipitated by conflicts. What these conflicts mean in marriages is that parents lack the skills necessary to resolve these conflicts. It may be pertinent for parents to learn skills necessary to resolve marital conflicts, thereby avoiding the possibility of divorce.

(6) There are licensed professionals who specialize in marriage counseling. It may be helpful to use the services of these professionals to help rethink divorce and seek alternatives.

(7) If divorce does happen, the well-being of your children should be paramount.

(8) If you are the parent ordered to pay child support, it is in the best interest of the children that you pay the child support as ordered. That money is intended to provide the necessities for your children. Avoiding payment is further hurting your children and exacerbating the pain and agony that your divorce already subjected them to.

(9) Custodial parents should be cooperative in allowing the parent paying child support to have access to the children insofar as visitation rights. There have been instances where a custodial parent refuses visitation in the name of anger and getting even.

LOVE AND MARRIAGE PERSPECTIVES

The children are the ones hurt most in these instances.

(10) The higher the degree of cooperation between a noncustodial father and a custodial mother, the fewer the deleterious effects of divorce on children. With such cooperation, the children tend to perceive the parents as still married, despite living in different households. Their sadness and their anger at their parents for divorcing are reduced. Their potential for acting-out behaviors is further lessened; as such cooperation enhances some resemblance of normalcy in the children's lives.

(11) Bitterness and anger between the divorced parents should be avoided as much as possible. Remember that both of you are divorced now. Anything both of you do at this point should be in the best interest of the children. Holding on to anger or bitterness causes people to be stuck. When you are stuck, you cannot move on with your life. If you are stuck and remarry, issues from your previous marriage follow you and, more often than not, affect your new marriage. It is not in your best interest to carry that excess baggage into your new marriage. The Bible advises that nobody puts a new wine into an old skin.

(12) There have been instances of divorced couples sneaking around and continuing to have sex with each other, even after remarriage. With this trend, is there any wonder that their prior marriage was in trouble in the first place? This is cheating, sex outside marriage, which is universally condemned in the scriptures.

(13) It may be a good idea for prospective couples to consider marriage preparation programs, where the benefits of marriage and the effects of divorce are discussed in detail prior to marriage. That may help potential couples think of the negative effects of divorce on their children and possibly reconsider before filing for divorce.

(14) Divorce imposes worries and responsibilities on children that may not be age-appropriate. Children sometimes think that it is their fault if their parents' divorce. As parents, we should not let them take responsibility for a divorce. The decision to divorce is strictly made by the adults in the marriage, not the children. It then follows that the responsibility for the divorce is on the adults and the adults alone.

(15) With divorce, some children become confused and even disoriented about what is going on with their parents. They may ask questions. It is the responsibility of both their parents to respond to their questions truthfully. Remember when answering questions that it is not the time to start telling them what a no-good parent their father or mother is.

(16) Children are sometimes torn in their loyalty between parents. It is best to make them understand that each parent loves them equally. Any post-divorce discord further hurts the children and complicates an already difficult situation. The coping and adjustment of the children should be paramount.

LOVE AND MARRIAGE PERSPECTIVES

(17) If the mother is the custodial parent, she may want to consider limiting the men that she brings into her household, her bedroom in particular. This requirement is the same if the father is the custodial parent. He should consider limiting the women that he brings home. This is because children learn by observation. I am not trying to suggest that the custodial mother or father should not have a life after divorce. She should, but the way she has that life is what counts. Children tend to mimic what they see.

(18) Again, God hates divorce. I am aware that I started by stating that God hates divorce. I want to close with it as well so that I can reiterate the point.

I'm an excellent housekeeper. Every time I get a divorce, I keep the house.

—Zsa Zsa Gabor

CHAPTER FIFTEEN

Forgiveness

Forgiveness is a funny thing. It warms the heart and cools the sting.

—William Arthur Ward

OUR LORD'S PRAYER states in part, "Forgive us our trespasses as we forgive those who trespass against us." That statement tends to suggest that we will trespass against others, and other people will trespass against us. Another implication of that statement is that when we trespass against those people, they should forgive us, just as we should forgive them when they trespass against us. A further derivative of that statement is that it is a fact that people will trespass against each other. It is therefore up to each other to learn how to react when trespassed against. So is forgiveness how to react when we are trespassed on ... or when we trespass against others? Is God giving us a mandate that we must forgive at all cost? Is forgiveness one part of the remedy when we trespass or are trespassed against? Is there a difference between forgiveness in general and forgiveness in marriage? Assuming there is, why is forgiveness in marriage different from other type of forgiveness? So what is forgiveness? Let us review what forgiveness is all about.

LOVE AND MARRIAGE PERSPECTIVES

What is forgiveness?

Forgiveness is a letting-go process that frees the person forgiving and the person being forgiven. Let us illustrate this by way of example. Michael and Emmanuel were great friends. They had always done things together. One day Emmanuel stopped talking and interacting with Michael. After about two months of no interacting, Michael came with a mutual friend, Benson, to see Emmanuel and ask why he had refused to talk to Michael. Emmanuel explained how he had always cared about Michael and had loaned him money at least fifteen different times, and that recently, prior to their not talking to each other, had been the first time ever asking Michael to loan him money. He'd wanted to use the money to buy medicine for his child. All he'd wanted to borrow was twenty dollars. He knew that Michael had the money, for he'd given Michael a ride the day before to cash a check for fifteen thousand dollars, which he'd received as a settlement for an accident he had a while back. Emmanuel stated that he had never charged Michael for gas or his time when he took him grocery shopping and to run other errands. He was so hurt by Michael's action that he'd wanted no part of him again.

Michael apologized for his actions, admitted that he was wrong by accepting responsibility, and never rationalized his actions. Emmanuel forgave him after that apology, and they resumed their friendship. Processing that situation with Benson, both Michael and Emmanuel stated that they felt as if a burden had been lifted off their shoulders—that their lives had been stuck, but now they could move. They further stated that they felt as if what was trapped inside them had been let go.

This shows how forgiveness frees up the person forgiving and the person being forgiven so they can move forward with their lives and make it through the letting-go process.

Definition of forgiveness

Definitions of forgiveness abound – there are as many as there are people trespassing and forgiving each other. The best two definitions of forgiveness that I found are those of Karen (2001, 5) while discussing the psychology in forgiving and not forgiving. I selected what I termed or perceived as a good definitions of forgiveness: "Forgiveness is an aspect of the workings of love. It can be a bridge back from hatred and alienation as well as liberation from two kinds of hell: bitterness and victimhood on one side; guilt, shame, and self-recrimination on the other. The wish to repair a wounded relationship, whether it takes the form of forgiveness, apology, or some other bridging gesture, is a basic human impulse. The need to forgive – which may grow out of understanding, gratitude, sympathy, regret over the hurt one has caused, or simply a wish to reunite – may be as strong as the need to be forgiven, even if it comes upon us more subtly."

LOVE AND MARRIAGE PERSPECTIVES

The logic of forgiveness

The scripture has a combination of turning the other cheek and a middle-of-the road approach regarding forgiveness. In some instances, forgiveness appears absolute and infinite. In one instance, Peter the Apostle asked:

> *Lord, how often shall my brother sin against me and I forgive him? Up to seven times?* (Matthew 18:21)

Peter probably was thinking that he scored a diplomatic coup d'état by thinking that Jesus would concur with that many times regarding forgiveness. Jesus, being a master of answers, said to him:

> *I do not say to you up to seven times, but up to seventy times seven.* (Matthew 18:22)

The logic of forgiveness became established when Jesus told a parable of a servant who owed his master but was unable to pay. His master was moved with compassion and forgave his debts when he fell down and asked his master for patience. The same forgiven servant would not forgive a fellow servant that owed him less than a fraction of what was forgiven him. To cap it off, he threw that fellow servant in jail for his inability to pay him. The forgiven servant was given a taste of his own medicine and delivered to the torturers until he paid all his dues. Jesus noted in that regard:

So My heavenly Father also will do to you if each of you, from his heart, does not forgive his brother his trespasses. (Matthew 18:35)

Other pertinent scriptures

Two other pertinent scriptures are worthy of mention in relation to forgiveness. It is imperative to state that most Biblical writings tend to make forgiveness contingent on forgiving the one that harmed or trespassed against you. In other words, if you forgive others, you will be forgiven. On the other hand, if you do not forgive, you may not be forgiven. This tends to lead to the question, is forgiveness a choice or something that must be done whether you like it or not? Before we delve into the answers to that question, what are those two important scriptures that relate to forgiveness? One stated:

If you have anything against anyone, forgive him that your Father in heaven may also forgive you your trespasses. But if you did not forgive, neither will your Father in heaven forgive your trespasses. (Mark 11:25–26)

The other stated:

Let all bitterness, wrath, anger, clamor, and evil speaking be put away from you, with all malice. And be kind to one another, tenderhearted, forgiving one another, even as God in Christ forgave you. (Ephesians 4:31–32)

The common denominator of the quoted scriptures is contingent on forgiving others so you may be forgiven. That takes us to the next issue. Is forgiveness a choice? Let us review that question.

Forgiveness as a choice

Some studies make a case for forgiveness as a choice. Others make the case that forgiveness is automatic and must be done at all costs, regardless of the situation. Some of those who argue for forgiveness being a choice at some point make a case for automatic forgiveness. Nevertheless, the position of this book is that we should forgive others, but the one who trespassed against you has to ask for that forgiveness, unless that forgiveness means nothing to the person being forgiven. In marital forgiveness, once certain conditions are met, the spouse who was trespassed against must forgive. I will enumerate those conditions later in this chapter.

In non-marital forgiveness, the choice to forgive or not to forgive is yours. It should be stated, however, that I have yet to see a reason why we should not forgive the trespass if the forgiveness was asked properly, with contrition and remorse. Even in the absence of the two key ingredients of contrition and remorse, you should still forgive for your own physical, emotional, and mental health. Remember that forgiving somebody does not necessarily mean that you are reconciled with him or her, unlike marital forgiveness, where reconciliation and restoration are imperative. The person's actions after you forgive are what will lead to reconciliation or restoration. Let us explore regular forgiveness and marital forgiveness.

Regular forgiveness versus marital forgiveness

I would be doing the reader of this book a disservice if I discussed forgiveness without narrowing it to marital forgiveness. Any type of relationship that warrants continuity, be it friendship, marital, or familial, depends on some type of forgiveness for that relationship to be sustained and continued. To assume otherwise is to feign ignorance of human psychology, frailty, and failures.

In marriage, couples share at the deepest levels; once marriage is consummated, the couple becomes one flesh. In that situation, the couple depends on each other and does things in unison. That is why any breach of that togetherness or trust hurts the other spouse to the fullest. The pain can be excruciating. If you are married and your spouse, who is supposed to be your other and better half, contravenes against the marriage covenant, it hurts to the highest degree. Can you imagine how Caesar felt when his best friend and right-hand man, Brutus, betrayed him? Now imagine the excruciating pain if it were his wife who did so.

The point here is to demonstrate the violation of the sacred bond that holds husband and wife together, especially because of marital infidelity by one spouse. We are going to create a scenario of an imaginary couple named Claudette and Stan to give an example of the mechanics of marital forgiveness. Now let us review the case of Claudette and Stan.

Marital forgiveness

Stan and Claudette have been married for seven years. Claudette was at the bus stop one day when an old acquaintance of hers, named Holland, disembarked from the bus. They talked for a while and renewed their acquaintance. This led to Holland and Claudette having an affair, despite their being married to their respective spouses. This affair continued for a year, until Stan found out. What should Stan do if Claudette wants to be forgiven? Should Stan forgive her?

Mechanism of marital forgiveness

The key thing about marital forgiveness is that there is no single or universal panacea for marital forgiveness, for each couple is different. The circumstances of their coming together are also different. Their personalities are also different. Their hurt tolerance is unique to them when compared to other couples. Remember that people marry for different reasons. Some readers might be saying that if they were Stan, they would walk away from the marriage, no questions asked. However, many factors come into play here. At this stage, we do not know if Claudette had had affairs previously in the marriage, or whether Stan had. What about how Stan feels about the marriage, his propensity to forgive, his hurt tolerance level, and other subtle factors that the scenario did not mention? Here is what I think should be the general rule for forgiveness ... or the steps to marital forgiveness.

Steps to marital forgiveness

The first thing that Claudette should do is ask this question: "Am I ready to discuss this issue?" By being ready, Claudette has to tackle this issue with Stan head-on. She should be open. She should not be defensive or try to rationalize. Claudette should be sincere and not withhold, for not being completely forthcoming will exacerbate the situation. She should not try to manipulate her way to forgiveness, which is why she should proceed only when she is ready to discuss the issue honestly. While discussing, she should show humility and a spirit of contrition.

Acknowledgment

The second stage is that she should acknowledge and admit what she did. In acknowledging, she should try not to sugarcoat it but be as forthcoming as possible. Remember the following:

> *A soft answer turns away wrath, but a harsh word stirs up anger.* (Proverbs 15:1)

If Stan thinks that he cannot handle the truth, then Claudette should be brief at the acknowledgment stage and move on to the next step. It is up to Stan, however, to advise her to skip to the next stage if he thinks that his anger will get the better part of him. It is said:

> *A wrathful man stirs up strife, but he who is slow to anger allays contention.* (Proverbs 15:18)

Taking responsibility

The next stage is the apology or responsibility stage. This is where Claudette apologizes for her actions and takes full and absolute responsibility. This is not the time to rationalize by taking partial responsibility and then telling Stan that he has not been giving her enough sex or a particular type of sex. That is why it is absolute responsibility, and Claudette should mean every word of it.

Asking for forgiveness

This is the stage for Claudette to ask Stan for forgiveness. She should do that wholeheartedly, boldly, and humbly. Remember:

> *Before honor is humility.* (Proverbs 15:33)

Now that Claudette has humbled herself by asking for forgiveness, Stan should honor her by forgiving her. Going through these stages demonstrates Claudette's remorsefulness. It is not easy to go through these stages, and you want a face-saving gesture for your wife. She may have cheated, but being humiliated in the process is another issue.

Why the husband must forgive

We used the case of Stan and Claudette as an example. It does not mean that wives are the only ones that have affairs in marriages; husbands also do. Assuming that the husband was the one who had the affair, he should follow the same steps Claudette did. The wife must also forgive him after he has shown remorse, taken responsibility, and asked for forgiveness.

Laurine (2008, 129) noted as follows regarding marital forgiveness: "They work to forgive each other for the daily small hurts and the occasional large ones as well. They recognize that we are all fallen people, and that their spouses are never going to be perfect. They work to understand each other's differences so that they can appreciate each other's strengths."

Here is the argument for forgiveness in marriage. Let us use the case of Stan and Claudette again since we are used to it, and for ease of flow of logic and presentation. Assuming that Stan and Claudette intend to remain in the marriage, the most sensible thing to do is to forgive. In the interest of the marriage, the mechanism for reconciliation should be set in motion. Take into account that forgiveness is different from reconciliation. If Stan does not forgive but still wants to remain in the marriage, there is no marriage as it used to be—at least not until he forgives. If he does not forgive, there will be no trust in that marriage. The fundamentals and foundation of that marriage are gone. Forgiveness is what will restore that foundation, and trust, which are necessary ingredients needed for marriage to function. So in this instance, it makes absolute sense to forgive. Supposing Stan was the one who had the affair and wanted to remain in the marriage, I know that he would like for Claudette to forgive him. We should be cognizant of treating others the way we want to be treated when it comes to forgiveness.

Once Stan forgives, he should forgive with his whole heart. It would be counterproductive for Stan to keep bringing up Claudette's infidelity, which he has forgiven, whenever they have other marital problems. Once you forgive, you should bury the issue; bringing it up will leave the marriage in a stuck mode, where it becomes impossible for the marriage to move on. In other words, once you forgive, you should let go. The only time it would be appropriate to bring that issue up again is if Claudette had another affair, whether with Holland or someone else. Her doing so would illustrate that Claudette learned nothing from her past mistakes.

Forgiveness should be grudgeless

In marriage, as stated, when you forgive, you should let go completely. In some instances, this may seem easier said than done. It is easier to forgive in marriage when the spouses involved are in love and their bonding is great and deep. Sometimes the amount of harm done comes into play, but with love, bonding, and the power of forgiveness, the couple should overcome. Every marriage sometimes goes through trials and tribulations, and forgiveness is one aspect of love that can repair the broken nuts and bolts of a relationship. It is like a bridge to somewhere—in this instance, to the hearts of the couples so they can see that bridge as a reconnecting conduit to their hearts.

When one spouse wants to remain in the marriage but doesn't feel obligated or want to forgive the other spouse, chances are that the unforgiving spouse has some anger issues that he or she needs to work on, probably through psychotherapy. Assuming that type of spouse forgives, he or she is likely to bear grudges and make the life of the other spouse miserable. Let us revisit the case of Stan and Claudette. Let us assume that Stan forgives but requires Claudette to take an HIV test every six months, because he cannot trust her. Stan may still be holding grudges. He may not see it that way, or may even deny that he is holding a grudge. Things like that can make Claudette cold and even make her withhold some of her loving by being sexually cold toward him. Stan can aggravate the situation during that sexual coldness by insinuating to Claudette that she is cold to him because he is not Holland. The point here is that when you forgive; do not hold grudges toward your spouse. Holding grudges will accomplish nothing. Grudges have the propensity to stagnate the marriage in such situations.

As stated earlier, no single strategy is a solution to all marriages, for each couple is different, as are their personalities. It is also further imperative to take into account the necessary and critical conditions for forgiveness to take place.

Regular forgiveness

It is for the respective individual to know at what point to forgive or not to forgive. For some people, forgiveness is instant, for others, it takes a lifetime. The relationship of the individuals involved as well as the intensity of the harm comes into play. Some people are more likely to forgive, while some people are less likely to forgive. So forgiveness depends on the individual, and how he or she wants to exercise the option of choosing to forgive. This is unlike marital forgiveness that is imperative to forgive, in that your spouse is part of you due to being one flesh. In marriage, there is so much at stake, such as children, emotional bonding, mortgages, and mutual investment of time and assets. There is also that phrase reminding us:

Forgive, and you will be forgiven. (Luke 6:37)

Conclusion

I will conclude this chapter on marital forgiveness by stating that your spouse is part of you. When you hurt your spouse, you are hurting yourself. Before doing anything that will impugn the integrity of your marriage, ask yourself if it is worth risking your marriage for whatever act you are contemplating. If after that contemplation, you did not resist that temptation, I hope that your spouse will understand human frailties. Taking human frailties into account, your spouse should consider this when it comes to forgiveness.

FORGIVENESS

On the contrary, you ought rather to forgive and comfort him, lest perhaps such a one be swallowed up with too much sorrow. Therefore I urge you to reaffirm your love to him. For to this end I also wrote that I might put you to the test, whether you are obedient in all things. Now whom you forgive anything, I also forgive. For if indeed I have forgiven anything, I have forgiven that one for your sakes in the presence of Christ, lest Satan take advantage of us; for we are not ignorant of his devices. (2 Corinthians 2:7–11)

Forgiveness does not change the past, but it does change the future.

—Paul Boese

Concluding Remarks

LOVE AND MARRIAGE technically mean different things to different people. The respective couples in a relationship know what their own definitions of love and marriage are. When couples bond at the dating stage, the foundation of their marriage is set at that time. The more chemistry the couple has, the more likely it is that their marriage will last. Skills are needed in choosing a mate, and it is not advisable to select any spouse that comes along without knowing that he or she has most of the attributes you want. It is pertinent to add that no spouse will have all the attributes that one needs, which is why it is good to prioritize and know what your top three to five attributes are.

Openness is a desired attribute in marriage. It helps marital communication flow with relative ease. Without communication, your marriage is doomed. In the rush to communicate your feelings with your spouse, it is imperative to listen actively. Without active listening, your communication is not effective, thereby defeating the purpose of it.

Marriage is like a garden—it needs maintenance to grow. When your marriage grows, the rewards are enriching, and the survival of that marriage is increased. Building a successful marriage

LOVE AND MARRIAGE PERSPECTIVES

requires the ability to compromise. An understanding that each other's needs are important in the relationship is desirable. The trend and the direction of the marital relationship depend on the couple in that marriage. Husband and wife should be willing to acknowledge and accept their own deficiencies and tolerate their mate's imperfections.

No marriage is immune to divorce. Our actions in the course of marriage can precipitate divorce. Our actions can also inhibit the chance of divorce. Our attitudes can make or break our marriages. Keeping a marriage together should be the objective of any married couple. Divorce should be avoided at any cost. God did not sanction divorce. Children are the ones mostly harmed by divorce. This is because their fathers and mothers can move on to other relationships and have some semblance of normalcy, while in some instances; the children are irretrievably harmed, which is a disastrous outcome.

Bibliography

Amato, P. R. 1993. "Children's Adjustment to Divorce: Theories Hypotheses and Empirical Support." *Journal of Marriage and Family* 55: 23–38.

Amato, P. R. 1994. "Father-Child Relations, Mother-Child Relations and Psychological Well-Being." *Marriage and the Family* 56:1031–1042.

Anderson, Thomas C., and Maureen Anderson. 2003. *Making Your Marriage a Love Story.* Mesa, AZ: WinWord Publishing, 7 and 177.

Bartos, Otomar J., and Paul Wehr. 2002. *Using Conflict Theory.* Cambridge, United Kingdom.

Bengtson, Vern, Timothy J. Biblarz, and Robert E. L. Roberts. 2002. *How Families Still Matter.* Cambridge, United Kingdom: Cambridge University Press.

Bernard, Jessie. 1981. "The Good-Provider: Its Rise and Fall." *American Psychologist* 36 (1): 1–12.

Berscheid, E., and H. T. Reis. 1998. "Attraction and Close Relationships." *The Handbook of Social Psychology* 2:193.

Booth, A. *Causes and Consequences of Parental Divorce: Reflections on Recent Research.* In Amato, P. R., and R. A. Thompson, eds., 1999. The Post- Divorce Family. Thousand Oaks, CA: Sage Publications.

Bumpass, L. L., and A. Sweet. December 1972. "Differentials in Marital Instability." *American Sociological Review* 37:754–766.

Buss, D. M. 1987. "Selection, Evocation and Manipulation." *Journal of Personality and Social Psychology* 53:1214–1221.

Byrne, D. "Attitudes and Attraction." In L. Berkowitz, ed., 1969. *Advances in Experimental Social Psychology* 4:36.

Cameron, Peter John. 2000. *Lord, Teach Us to Pray: The What and How of Prayer.* New Haven, CT: Knights of Columbus.

Caspi, A., and E. E. Herbener. 1990. "Continuity and Change: Assortative Marriage and Consistency of Personality in Adulthood." *Journal of Personality and Social Psychology* 58:250–258.

Chapman, Gary D. 2005. *The Four Seasons of Marriage.* Wheaton, IL: Tyndale House Publishers, Inc.

Cherlin, A. August 1977. "The Effects of Children on Marital Dissolution." *Demography* 14:265–272.

Cherlin, A. J. 1978. Remarriage as an incomplete institution. *American Journal of Sociology* 84: 634–650.

Furstenberg, F. F. Jr., and C. W. Nord. 1985. "Parenting Apart: Patterns of Childrearing After Marital Disruption." *Journal of Marriage and the Family* 47:893–904.

Gibbs, Nancy. 2009. "What Women Want Now: A Time Special Report." *Time*, October, 26 25–33.

Glick, Paul C. 1988. "Fifty Years of Family Demography: A Record of Social Change." *Journal of Marriage and the Family* 50 (4): 868.

Gould, R. E. 1974. *Measuring Masculinity by Size of a Paycheck: Men and Masculinity.* Englewood Cliffs, NJ: Prentice-Hall.

Hall, D., and F. Hall. 1979. *The Two-Career Couples.* Reading, MA: Addison-Wesley.

Hochschild, Arlie Russell. 1989. *The Economy of Gratitude.* Greenwich, CT: JAI Press, 1989.

Karen, Robert. 2001. *The Forgiving Self.* New York: Doubleday.

Kelley; Harold H., John G. Holmes, Norbert L. Kerr, Harry T. Reis, Cary L. E. Rusbult, and Paul A. M. Van Lange. 2003. *An Atlas of Interpersonal Situations.* Cambridge, United Kingdom: Cambridge University Press.

Komarovsky, M. 1940. *The Unemployed Man and His Family.* New York: Dryden Press.

Laurine, Greg. 2008. *Becoming One.* New York: Faith Words, Hachette Book Group.

Lepine, Bob. 1999. *The Christian Husband.* Ann Arbor, MI: Servant Publication.

McLanahan, S. S., and G. Sandefur. 1994. *Growing up with a Single Parent: What Hurts, What Helps.* Cambridge, MA: Harvard University Press.

Pols, Mary. 2009. "Lost at Sea." *Time November,* 174 (17): 74.

Popenoe, David. 1990. *Family Decline in America, Rebuilding the Nest.* Milwaukee, WI: Family Service America.

Qian, Z. C. 1998. "Changes in Assortative Mating: The Impact of Age and Education, 1970–1990." *Demography* 35:279–292.

Random House Webster's Dictionary. 4th ed. New York: Random House.

Rosenbaum, M. E. 1986. "The Repulsion Hypothesis: On the Nondevelopment of Relationships." *Journal of Personality and Social Psychology* 51:1156–1166.

Rusbult, C. E., and Martz, J. M. 1995. "Remaining in an Abusive Relationship: An Investment Model Analysis of Non-Voluntary Commitment." *Personality and Social Psychology Bulletin* 21: 558–571.

Scanzoni, J. H. 1975. *Sex Roles, Life and Childbearing: Changing Patterns in Marriage and the Family.* New York: Free Press.

Stains, Roy, and Stefan Bechtel. 2000. *What Women Want.* New York: Rodale Publishing.

Strong, James. 2001. *Exhaustive Concordance of the Bible.* Grand Rapids, MI: Zondervan.

Trent, John, and Larry Weeden. 2006. *Breaking the Cycle of Divorce.* Carol Steam, IL: Tyndale House Publishers.

Invitation To Participate In Next Project

I AM CURRENTLY working on my next project, which involves cheating in relationships. I would like your input. If you would like to contribute to this project, I would appreciate your opinions as to the following:

- Why do people cheat in relationships?

- Who cheats more in relationships, men or women?

- If men cheat more, why?

- If women cheat more, why?

Please include your first name only to ensure confidentiality. You do not have to respond to all the questions, but it would be appreciated if you would. Send your answers, comments, or even questions to www.vincevincents.com. If you prefer, please e-mail me at www.vince@vincevincents.com. Absolute confidentiality and anonymity guaranteed. If you have any comment about cheating in relationships that is not stated above, it would be greatly welcomed. Some comments may be published. Thank you so much for your participation.

CPSIA information can be obtained at www.ICGtesting.com
229024LV00001B/42/P